Ropes, Reins, and Rawhide

All About Rodeo

MELODY GROVES

UNIVERSITY OF NEW MEXICO PRESS   ALBUQUERQUE

12 11 10 09 08 07 06   1 2 3 4 5 6 7

Library of Congress Cataloging-in-Publication Data

Groves, Melody, 1952–
    Ropes, reins, and rawhide : all about rodeo / Melody Groves.— 1st ed.
        p. cm.
    Includes index.
    ISBN-13: 978-0-8263-3822-8 (cloth : alk. paper)
    ISBN-10: 0-8263-3822-4 (cloth : alk. paper)
    1. Rodeos. I. Title.
    GV1834.G76 2006
    791.84—dc22
                            2006001054

Design and compostition: Melissa Tandysh

Contents

Foreword and Acknowledgments

Innumerable people and countless hours of hard work go into preparing for a rodeo. Competitors, producers, entertainers, and animals live for the thrills and spills associated with this heart-stopping event. Rodeo is a team effort. And just like putting on a rodeo, this book is a team effort too. Therefore, it's close to impossible to mention everyone who helped with research, insight, encouragement, permission, editing, enthusiasm, entry, and just plain help.

Putting this book together has been a wild ride, and I wish for you, the reader, to come join me. Enjoy the rodeo. There's nothing else like it.

My sincerest thanks to the world's best photographers:

Myke Groves   Bert Entwistle
Haley Crawford   Bob Willis

Extra special thanks to those who gave advice and their time:

Margaret Dean   Kelly Timberman
Casper Baca   Billy Etbauer

Charmayne James

Dennis Johnson

Gary Morton

Hadley Barrett

Luke Branquinho

Monty Lewis

Rich Skelton

Rob Smets

Speed Williams

Charlie Sampson

J. W. Kinder

Larry Lancaster

Martin Encinias

Kyle Encinias

Vernon Honeyfield

Mavrick Parrish

Michael Vigil

Mike Moore

Tony Garritano

Ann Blickert

Bill Blackwood

Burr Gagan

Theresia Gagan

C. J. Schwartz

Denise Abbott

Diane Christensen

Edna Mae Holden

Judy Avila

Judy Davis

Keith Pyeatt

Lincoln Bramwell

Linda Salomone

Marian Ray

Phil Jackson

Sue Brown

Luther Wilson

Fig. Intro.1.
This ranch rodeo bronc rider focuses on the horse's shoulders to keep his seat for the eight seconds.
PHOTO BY BERT ENTWISTLE.

Introduction

Heart pounding, blood pumping, the cowboy nods, chute gate opens and his world begins. Eight seconds of adrenaline rush. Eight seconds of gripping, pulling, and holding on. The animal under him bucks and twists attempting to dislodge the cowboy's seat but the rider sticks like glue. The buzzer sounds, the cowboy dismounts, tips his hat to a cheering crowd and nods at his proud fellow riders. Just another day at the office.

Originating from real ranch work, rodeo has few, but confusing rules. In this man against beast arena, the players are many and varied, ranging from the two-footed variety to the four-legged creatures.

This book explains the ins and outs and yes, ups and downs, of this exhilarating, extreme sport called *rodeo*.

Fig. 1.1.
Introduced by Spaniards coming up through Mexico, horses charged
their way into the American West and forever changed the West's future.
PHOTO BY HALEY CRAWFORD.

History of Rodeo

The word *rodeo* comes from the Spanish word "rodear"—to surround.
—William Manns, western author

RODEO. The quintessential extreme sport. The ultimate sport. A sport born in the wilds of the American West.

Then

To understand rodeo requires understanding a bit of American history. Rodeo today has come a long way since its humble beginnings in the American West. During the later 1700s and early 1800s, Spain controlled most of the land now considered the Southwest. Men called conquistadors dominated Texas, New Mexico, Arizona, and parts of California.

Established missions raised cattle for America's booming markets. The need grew for skilled horsemen to handle cattle and manage the herds. Many of the men running the missions were of Spanish nobility, trained in horsemanship and roping. This expertise was passed on to their workers, known as "vaqueros."

During Mexico's rule, the vaqueros found work running cattle and managing the rangeland. Even after the United States gained control of the Southwest in 1854, through the Gadsden Purchase, the vaqueros continued to work and teach their American counterparts. Their great horsemanship traditions propelled today's rodeo.

With the ending of the Civil War, cattle herds spread throughout the West and proportionally the number of cowboys grew. Once or twice a year, cowhands rounded up the cattle on the open range and drove them hundreds of miles to various market centers (stockyards).

In celebration of their job completed, the cowboys informally competed in challenges ranging from rope throwing to "cutting" cattle (isolating one cow from the rest of the herd). Spectators would inevitably gather to watch these rough and tough men show off their prowess.

Formal rodeo started with friendly competition between ranches when the work was done. Since cowboying tended to be a lonely job, the men were anxious to socialize and show off their abilities.

Beginning in the 1880s, the railroad arrived across the West, thus replacing the necessity of time-consuming cattle drives. Open rangeland became defined by barbed-wire fencing, thereby drastically cutting the number of cowhands. Many cowboys were forced to find a new way to make a living.

Although Deer Trail, Colorado, lays claim to the first rodeo in 1869, the first truly formal rodeo was held in Cheyenne, Wyoming, in 1872. Between 1890 and 1910, rodeo emerged as public entertainment through various Wild West Shows and Fourth of July celebrations. Buffalo Bill Cody, Wild Bill Hickok, Annie Oakley, and others promoted the enchantment of the Wild West and the thrill of rodeo as far away as Europe.

Not until the first decades of the twentieth century, however, did rodeo become recognized as a competitive sport. Annual stampedes, roundups and frontier days' events attracted regional audiences. It became a true spectator sport.

Trick riding and fancy roping were a popular part of rodeo from 1910 until the early 1930s, when their status switched from contested events to contract entertainment. The trick-riding contestants combined daring, acrobatic skills, superb timing, and real showmanship. They performed dangerous stunts like crupper somersaults or handstands while moving around the area on a loping horse. Fancy roping came from the *charro* riders of Old Mexico, such as Vincente Oropeza, who in 1894 introduced the *floreo de reata*, making flowers of rope.

By the mid-1920s, championship events at Boston Garden and New York City's Madison Square Garden attracted a nationwide focus.

The Rodeo Association of America (RAA), founded in 1929, combined a group of managers with promoters and gave structure to the rodeo. The RAA sanctioned events, selected judges, and established purse awards and point systems to determine all-around winners. Since 1946, the organization has acted as the International Professional Rodeo Association (IPRA).

Until 1936, rodeo contestants themselves remained unorganized. Then a group formed the Cowboy Turtle Association (CTA) so named because they were "slow" to

Fig. 1.2.
Reata, fancy ropework with roots in Spain, still delights today's rodeo spectators.
Photo by Haley Crawford.

Fig. 1.3.
Nationally ranked New Mexico State University Rodeo Team practices barrel racing.
PHOTO BY AUTHOR.

organize but finally "stuck their necks out" for what they believed in. In 1945, the CTA became the Rodeo Cowboys Association (RCA), renamed in 1975 the Professional Rodeo Cowboys Association (PRCA).

Women who compete in rodeo formed their own organization, Women's Professional Rodeo Association (WPRA), which includes all of rodeo's regular events except saddle bronc riding. Professional Women's Rodeo Association (PWRA), a sister organization, is limited to female roughstock riders only. Rodeo cowgirls were among the first women in the United States to achieve recognition as professional athletes. By 1920, women had achieved a prominent place in rodeo as roughstock riders, trick riders, and relay racers.

However, beginning in the 1930s, competitive cowgirls declined in number and prominence. Male-dominated rodeo organizations ignored women as serious contenders and instead opted for the glamorous but nonathletic "Ranch Girls." With

Gene Autry's monopoly of big-time rodeo in the 1940s, the place of female contestants virtually disappeared.

Women are finally making a comeback in rodeo, but in small measures. The exception is barrel racing, where women rule.

Now

Most major rodeos fall under the jurisdiction of the PRCA, headquartered in Colorado Springs, Colorado. A rodeo boasts standardized events including bareback riding, saddle bronc riding, steer wrestling, calf roping, barrel racing, and the ever-popular bull riding.

Bull riding has become so popular that in 1992 a group of bull riders formed the Professional Bull Riders (PBR). This association is headquartered in Colorado Springs, Colorado but will be moving to Albuquerque, New Mexico in the near future.

Fig. 1.4.
Calf roping is a ranch chore now featured in rodeo.
Photo by author.

With the exception of bull riding, all events in rodeos come directly off every-day ranch work. For example, calves need to be dehorned, doctored, vaccinated, or otherwise tended by the ranch hands. Two cowboys rope the calf while another cowhand performs whatever needs to be done. When a cowboy needs to catch a calf, he and his horse work together to capture the speedy youngster. This led to team roping in rodeo.

Rodeo, the most extreme of extreme sports, is highly popular in the United States and Canada. More than two thousand rodeos are held annually in those countries. Brazil, Mexico, and Australia are steadily increasing their fascination of rodeo. It is estimated that over twenty-two million spectators flock to the rodeos annually.

Ranking contestants usually compete in more than 120 rodeos per year for total prize money in excess of twenty-six million dollars. They strive for the pinnacle of success—the Wrangler National Finals, which offers an additional three million dollars in prize monies.

Fig. 1.5.
Rodeo animals receive top care. The padded breast collar and cinch provide extra comfort for the horse. A happy animal performs well.
Photo by author.

Rodeo is divided into two categories: 1) Those scored by a judge (roughstock events); and 2) Those timed for speed (barrel racing, tie-down roping, team roping, and steer wrestling). The contests of riding and roping require only two things of the horses and cattle—either to buck or to run, and both are natural.

Animal Treatment

Rodeo associations around the country have strict rules that dictate how contests may be conducted and the animals handled. In 1947, the Professional Rodeo Cowboys Association established rules for the humane care and treatment of rodeo animals— seven years before the founding of the Humane Society of the United States.

Injury to animals is infrequent with rates documented as low as 1 percent. In 2000, during 72,000 animal performances, there were 308 injuries, which equates to .000054. The cowboys' statistics are not nearly as impressive.

The use of horses and bulls in rodeo is so undemanding that they stay healthy and perform well past their natural life span. Veterinarians attribute their longevity to the excellent feed and adequate exercise.

Spurs, used by bull and bronc riders, are equipped with blunted rowels (the round part of the spur) and do not hurt the animal.

Flank straps, which encircle the animal in the flank area, are fleece lined and do *not* cover genitalia or cause pain. If the strap were too tight, the animal would simply refuse to move, much less buck.

Many people are not aware of the price of rodeo animals. Recently, a bull was purchased at the Wrangler National Finals Rodeo for well over eighty thousand dollars. Good roping horses sell for fifty thousand dollars. Who isn't going to take real good care of those animals? Every year, various rodeo associations give honors to the best performing horses and bulls and present awards to the owners.

Rodeos

Leading rodeos today include Frontier Days in Cheyenne, Wyoming; Wrangler National Finals Rodeo in Las Vegas; Professional Bull Riding Finals also held in Las Vegas; National Western Stockshow and Rodeo in Denver, Colorado; Houston Livestock Show and Rodeo in Houston, Texas; and the Calgary Stampede in Calgary, Alberta, Canada.

Fig. 2.1.
Stock contractor Casper Baca helps out at the chutes.
PHOTO BY AUTHOR.

2

Stock Contractors and Animals: Without Them, Ain't No Rodeo

My heart's in rodeo—everything I do is rodeo.
—Casper Baca, stock contractor

"IT'S THE BRONCS and the blood, it's the steers and the mud . . . and they call the thing *rodeo*," explains a classic country tune sung by Garth Brooks. Rodeo is a sport that combines the athleticism of man and beast. And at the heart of wrangling that "beast" is the stock contractor. Without these men, whose lives revolve around horses, bulls, and cattle, rodeo could not exist.

What Is a Stock Contractor?

"Stock is the basis of your business," states Grants, New Mexico, stock contractor Casper Baca. Men who love animals raise horses, bulls, steers, and calves. No one could spend the millions of hours caring for these four-legged critters and not love the life. Stock contractors, the coaches of the rodeo world, provide the animals for the rodeos.

When a rodeo committee sets a date for a rodeo, they contact one or more contractors who then figure out how many of which kind of animals are needed. The stock contractor then sorts through his herd and selects the proper four-legged athlete. According to Baca, he picks his animals based on how far his stock must travel: "Some are good at short distances, others can take a long haul."

After arriving at the rodeo site, the contractor makes sure his animals are fed and watered before he is. After the rodeo, he is in charge of properly and safely loading the truck, then hauling his animals back home.

The Stock

Livestock—horses, both bucking and saddle broke; bulls; steers; and calves—must live somewhere and what better place than a ranch? Baca's 120 horses spend the winter in central New Mexico, out in the pasture, while his 60 bulls winter in feed lots. Typical of the life of rodeo animals, Baca's horses and bulls enjoy weeks of nothing but eating, sleeping, and an occasional sparring match with other pasturemates. A bull's bucking ability peaks at around eight years of age, and a horse's around twelve. However, both can buck for several years after that.

Contractors bring saddle-broke horses for the rodeo queens, pick up men, or just as a "spare." For the timed events—team and calf roping, steer wrestling—the

Fig. 2.2.
Good stock allows the competitor a chance to win that gold buckle.
PHOTO BY AUTHOR.

Fig. 2.3.
At this Belen, New Mexico, roughstock rodeo, the
bucking horses run in the arena before performing.
PHOTO BY AUTHOR.

steers are neutered yearling males weighing between 500 and 650 pounds and both horns must be at least eight inches long. The calves must be weaned from their mothers and weigh between 220 and 280 pounds. These timed-event animals must be uniform in size and temperament, thus ensuring the contestants of equal opportunity to score points.

Team ropers, calf ropers, and steer wrestlers usually bring their own horses.

While Baca does not spend much time with a breeding program, preferring instead to buy proven good bucking stock, other contractors, such as Dillon and H. D. Page of D&H Cattle Company, have developed a top bucking bull breeding program. Many of their bulls originate from the famous Plummer bloodlines. Contractor and breeder Ronnie Roach bought many Plummers, and today a few of the original bulls sporting the "CP" (Charlie Plummer) brand are still around.

Around 1963, Charlie Plummer of Sayer, Oklahoma, bought his first set of bulls and cows from Tom Harlan of Texas. Plummer started putting on rodeos with the bulls of this lineage and discovered their tremendous bucking ability. These bulls and their descendants would become legends for their bad temperament and superb bucking ability. Known as "Plummers," many of them are on the "small-ish" side (twelve hundred pounds), white with black spots. Their horns tend to be big.

Many of the world-famous bulls bucking in the Professional Bull Riders (PBR) and Professional Rodeo Cowboys Association (PRCA) rodeos can trace their ancestry back to Plummer bulls. In 1985 Dillon and H. D. Page purchased bucking heifers (one dollar per pound) with Plummer bloodlines.

Bucking horses, like bulls, are not taught to buck; it's a trait that is bred into them. Bucking is not inherent to one or two particular breeds, but rather to the genetic lineage. Some contractors breed horses, but others, like Casper Baca, prefer to purchase proven stock.

A mix of Shire, Percheron, and Thoroughbred combine the qualities of sturdiness with agility and speed in horses. While breeding programs continue to create good bucking stock, some horses come from unknown lineage but for some reason cannot be trained to ride with saddles. Stock contractors are always on the lookout for a horse that's hard to ride.

Awards are given to outstanding stock and contractors at the annual Wrangler National Finals Rodeo (WNFR) and PBR Finals. Dillon and H. D. Page have won the coveted PBR World Championship Stock Contractor Award for 2001, 2002, 2003, 2004, and 2005. The top forty-five bull riders in the world, which makes the honor very special, vote on this award. "The award shows the caliber and quality of the stock," says Casper Baca.

Quality stock brings quality prices for the contractor. When a bull wins the coveted PBR Bull of the Year award, his owner now has a prize-winning bull that will fetch high prices—if he chooses to sell. At the 2004 World Finals Bull Sale in Las Vegas, Nevada, a two-year-old bull of D&H Cattle Company sold for twenty thousand dollars and Salt River Rodeo Bulls' Midnight Confessions fetched fifty-four thousand dollars. And that bull didn't even have a blue ribbon tucked under one hoof. In recent years, an outstanding bucking bull sold for eighty thousand dollars.

Preparing for the Rodeo

Long before the stock contractor gets that call from the rodeo committee, he must prepare his stock to perform their best during the rodeo. This is no small feat. To begin, a two-year-old bull, too young to buck with a person on board, is outfitted with a mechanical "dummy," a small box with antennae on top designed to simulate a human rider. The dummy is programmed to come off the bull after six seconds. Around the age of three, if the contractor deems his bull to be strong enough, a live rider will sit on top of the animal.

Once the animals are used to being around people, they are introduced to the rodeo chutes, the iron maze of pipes behind the fences. They have to learn how to line up, take their turn in the boxes (the chutes that open into the arena), and how to load into a truck. This is practiced many times before a contractor will spend the time and money taking a new horse or bull to a rodeo.

Baca explains the basics of stock contracting. If the contractor brings an animal that doesn't perform, not only does the rider not get points (which translates into money), the audience gets bored. Worst of all, the contractor may not be hired by

Fig. 2.4.
Healthy stock bucks high and gives this cowboy a ride he won't soon forget.
PHOTO BY MYKE GROVES.

that rodeo committee again. Every animal has an off day, but consistently poor bucking stock will break a contractor's business.

To ensure good bucking, Baca stresses, contractors must tend to their animals first. Good feed, medical care, and proper handling of the animals are paramount. A happy bull is a bucking bull.

Feed for horses and bulls is the main part of his expenses, says contractor Casper Baca. But, since livestock is the basis for business, he admits, it's money well spent. "You gotta feed them good." Average cost is three dollars a head per day. Each horse is given ten pounds of grain every day, after being fed thirty to forty pounds of hay (one-half bale). The grain is a healthy mixture of corn, barley, molasses, alfalfa, oats, ground hay, cottonseed hulls, and silage. Some contractors use old cereal, discarded by cereal companies. Combined with ground hay, the animals take to the treat just like kids.

Horses' digestive systems are tender, so finding the right combination of food for them is tricky. And just like people, each horse is different. Colic is the number one threat to a horse's health. Severe colic, brought on by any number of things including a new food, sand (ingested when munching on grass), or even stress, can cause death.

Bulls, on the other hand, are much stronger and can eat a wide variety of feeds without showing any adverse signs. However, wet, new hay will bloat bulls. New feed products, such as Bucker's Blend, are designed to provide bucking bulls with the nutrients needed to heft their poundage during a rodeo.

In order to haul animals to rodeos, contractors must have veterinarian approval and signed forms identifying the animals in addition to certificates verifying their good health. Brands are the best way to identify animals, and in addition to the owner's brand, often the animal's number must be added. This keeps animal confusion to a minimum. For example, if two black bulls have the same name (all rodeo stock have names), the only way a contestant can be sure he rides the correct one is the number on the bull's side. For competition in the PBR, bulls must be number branded as well.

When crossing state borders, the contractors are responsible to demonstrate proper and safe hauling of these animals if the transportation authorities ask. He must know how many pounds each axle can carry and the maximum weight allowed on the road. He's also responsible for shifting the stock around if they move during the transport.

At the Rodeo

Once the animals arrive at the rodeo arena, usually a day ahead of the event, Baca tallies the chores waiting before unloading the stock. First and foremost on the list is making sure all gates are closed. The mental image of loose horses and bulls, glad to be out of the confines of the trailer and running amok throughout the area, is at the front of the contractor's mind. Those gates are closed tight before any animal is released.

Second chore is to locate the water troughs, then make sure feed is available. Last is checking the facility to get a good layout of the area. Then, and only then, are the animals unloaded from the trailer.

They are herded back to the watering station, usually located in the back of the chutes, where the contractor checks the health of each and every animal. Some livestock experience "car sickness" and need extra TLC for a few minutes after unloading. Baca stresses that horses and bulls that don't travel well will only be good for short distances, and may have to be sold to rodeo companies that send stock just a few miles down the road. Livestock must be hardy travelers, as the animals spend hours in the trailer going from state to state. "If they can take the hauling and still buck—they're good."

Fig. 2.5.
Eighteen wheelers transport livestock from rodeo to rodeo.
Photo by Myke Groves.

Livestock is sorted in holding pens. Who goes where depends on the animal's personality. "There's always a pecking order," says Baca. "Some horses are just mean-natured, and some are wimpy." And some bulls get along well with others, and some can't play in the sandbox at all. It's up to the contractor to sort them out.

The day of the rodeo is exciting not just for the contractor, who has a myriad of things to do, but for the animals themselves. With every new person who comes into the arena area, the animals can sense the growing excitement. Horses keep their ears forward in anticipation. Feed before the rodeo is light. Just like human athletes, animals that are overfed can't perform to their best ability. A light snack prior to the event works well.

The stock contractor himself must be a man of many talents and be every-where at once. He must take final stock of his animals, then sort them in order of

Fig. 2.6.
After spending several hours cooped up in the truck, the animals enjoy milling around in the pens waiting for their chance to put a cowboy on his pockets.
Photo by author.

Fig. 2.7.
Casper Baca lends a hand while doling out advice to his cowboys.
PHOTO BY AUTHOR.

competition. In roughstock events, the bucking horses are always first in line. Then the saddle broncs, then the bulls. In regular rodeo, it's still the bareback horses first. Bulls are last—this event keeps the spectators glued to their seats.

In addition to checking on the animals, the stock contractor is busy giving advice to the competitors, identifying which animal does what. "He's gonna go out and jump left, then spin—most times." Usually a former rodeo rider himself, the contractor often finds himself a guide or mentor to younger riders. It's also the contractors behind the chutes who cheer and yell encouragement to the rider during the eight-second ride. More excitement leads to better rides, which leads to more audience enjoyment. And that's what this game is all about: enjoyment.

The stock contractor's role, according to Casper Baca, is "to put on a first class rodeo. You have a commitment to the rodeo committee, the riders, and the audience." The riders need and deserve quality stock, and the audience deserves fast-paced entertainment. "Give them their money's worth."

Baca, also a rodeo producer, hires the arena personnel—the pick up men, announcers, timers, judges, secretaries, and clowns, in addition to contracting with other livestock owners for steers and calves. Indeed, a man of many talents.

After the Rodeo

Lights are out, buckles and saddles awarded, the audience has gone home. But not the stock contractor and his animals. He still has to sort and pen and feed and water and check his stock again. The stock now receives plenty of grain and water. "Horses will work for food," Baca says with a chuckle.

Oftentimes, the stock and contractor stay overnight, resting up for the next day's ride home. Baca explains that if he has less than two hundred miles and it's still daylight, he may haul his animals on home. But if it's more miles and/or night, he waits until everyone is rested. He puts as little stress as possible on his stock.

When he decides the animals are ready, the contractor loads his animals and drives home, planning for the next rodeo.

So You Want to Be a Stock Contractor?

Stock contracting is an expensive business. In addition to the initial cost of buying an animal, its feed, veterinarian care, livestock inspection, licensing, and rodeo transportation adds up exponentially. The average purchase cost for a bucking horse is twenty-five hundred dollars and for a bull thirty-five hundred dollars.

Equipment is expensive, too. Baca, like many contractors, uses trailers with aluminum floors. The wooden floors wear through and break after repeated use. Good pickup trucks used for hauling hay and smaller stock trailers are essential to contractors. After each trip, the trailers must be cleaned out to help keep the stock healthy. Of course, insurance, good tires, and regular mechanical maintenance are required. Contractors, along with other arena personnel, may bring a small travel trailer and park it on or near the rodeo grounds. This system works well when hauling family, too.

Baca advises anyone interested in becoming a stock contractor to take it slow. It requires time (and money) to buy good stock. Breeding takes years. He also stresses learning about the animals, especially for someone who has little or no ranching background. His best advice, he says, "is to be as honest as you can." He maintains that treating people well, contestants and audience alike, is the key to a successful business.

"There's a lot of traveling in it. You're not in the same place every time." Baca has lost track of how many thousands of miles he's hauled his stock since going into business in 1986. Looking back and thinking of how far he's come since then, he smiles. "I have no regrets."

"It's the boots and the chaps, it's the cowboy hats . . . it's spurs and latigo. It's the ropes and the reins, the joy and the pain . . . and they call the thing *rodeo*." Thank you, Garth Brooks.

3

Announcers and Other
Really Important People

I take the mystery out of rodeo. I guide the
audience to what the riders are doing.
—Hadley Barrett, Hall of Fame announcer

THINK RODEO—bucking animals, brave cowboys, cheering crowds. But it takes more than one horse, one man, and a few spectators to make a rodeo. Behind the scenes, behind the chutes, and behind the microphones are the people who make rodeo happen.

Announcers

The voice of rodeo, the connection between the contestants and spectators, is the announcer. His job, according to announcers Hadley Barrett (1999 Hall of Fame inductee) and J. W. Kinder, is to guide the audience as to what the cowboys are doing. They educate, inform, and yes, entertain. Kinder stresses that his job as announcer is to inform, not *perform*.

Fig. 3.1.
Hall of Fame announcer Hadley Barrett explains ranch rodeo procedures during the Ranch Rodeo Championship Finals in Amarillo, Texas.
PHOTO BY MYKE GROVES

Fig. 3.2.
Announcer J. W. Kinder looks out the announcer's booth watching the action below.
PHOTO BY AUTHOR.

Announcers know the sport, most of them having been roughstock riders themselves. This gives them the advantage of knowing, firsthand, what it's like to ease
down onto the bull. The adrenaline pumping, the breath caught in the rider's chest.
A good announcer, according to Barrett, "finds out who these contestants are, then
tells the crowd." Often, they spend an hour or two before the rodeo talking to the
riders. Kinder reports that just as often, riders come to him with information.

Reading the audience takes practice, but both Barrett and Kinder say that listening to the oohs and aahs during the first few bareback rides lets them know
the experience level of the audience. Seasoned rodeo fans know what to look for
and react to the cowboy's rides. Novice fans holler at wild rides, the more flash and
dash the better. In addition, Barrett notes that when announcing a ranch rodeo, he
realizes that a large percentage of his audience knows what they're looking at, so
he gears his information more toward the riders themselves rather than spending
more time on the rules and event description.

Barrett's choice of words changes daily, especially when he announces an event that lasts more than two days. His audience becomes accustomed to phrases (like "down too soon," "lifts the latch"), so he must find phrases that mean the same thing.

"I want my audience to know, when they walk out, what happened," announcer Kinder explains. "Of those first timers, ninety-seven percent will return if you make it fun for them." He makes sure the audience follows along with the scoring as well as giving updates on riders' injuries.

Announcers attend rodeo school, much like the contestants. The announcer school is a four-day workshop that includes how to explain the events, rodeo terminology, what to say when a rider's hurt, and how to transition from second to second while keeping the audience's interest. Toward the end of the school, they announce a mock rodeo where the events are on television.

Announcers—interpreters, educators, entertainers. They do it all.

Pick Up Men

Pick up men are just that—men on horseback who offer a helping hand to bronc riders after the eight-second buzzer sounds. "Our main job is safety," says Belen, New Mexico, pick up man Martin Encinias. "Safety for the rider and the animal."

Like the bullfighter saving a cowboy, the pick up men take care of a rider and the horse. Good pick up men are experienced horsemen, familiar with all kinds of livestock. "You gotta know how to ride a horse," Encinias says. "You gotta be a cowboy, in the saddle every day, gotta be able to read a horse's mind." Pick up men learn to anticipate the animal's movement as well as the rider's.

Encinias and his son, Kyle, a pick up man for two years, stress that to be successful, timing is everything. They must know how to "sandwich" a rider between their horses, allowing the cowboy to grab onto the nearest one.

Once that chute gate opens, the pick up men go on high alert. "We watch the rider and try to stay out of the judge's way." In order to help the horse buck its best, pick up men slap their chaps, whooping and hollering, making noise to help keep the horse focused on bucking. When the buzzer sounds at eight seconds, the pick up men swoop in to offer assistance to the rider. "We ask, 'Are you out?'" meaning, Is the rider's hand out of the grip? Encinias says that if the answer is yes, he steers as close as he can so the contestant can make a grab for him. Riders launch themselves off the bronc and grab anything close by. If the answer is no, Encinias figures out the problem and barks orders to the other pick up man as well as the rider. Safety for humans and animals is his number one job.

As soon as the rider is off the horse, the pick up men gallop next to the bronc, which can run as fast as thirty miles an hour, then grab the bronc's hack rein. They then must maneuver around in order to release the flank strap. Once it's off, usually the horse calms down to the point where the pick up men can direct it toward the holding pens. They don't want the animal to injure itself, which could happen by stepping on a dragging rein. Tangled legs could result in a cartwheel across the arena, a broken leg or neck, or scrapes and bruises for both men and horse.

Pick up men also help a rider break free who's become entangled in the reins or whose spur is caught in a cinch strap. They help get him loose the quickest way possible, no matter how tight the situation might be. Safety for everyone is at the front of the pick up man's mind. "You never know what's gonna happen," says the 1999 Navajo Nation Pick up Man of the Year, Martin Encinias.

Injuries to pick up men don't happen often, but when they do, they can be severe—broken bones from falls and tangled horses, deep bruises from kicks, and thumbs cut off. Encinias wears shin guards under his smooth chaps, which are padded with an inch and a half of foam. If a bucking bronc kicks up, he can avoid, or at least reduce, severe bruises or broken bones.

Fig. 3.3.
A pick up man rushes in to help a cowboy off his bucking horse.
PHOTO BY MYKE GROVES

Fig. 3.4.
Two pick up men sandwich the horse and cowboy
between them, allowing the rider a chance to dismount.
PHOTO BY MYKE GROVES.

Kyle Encinias reports that the pick up horse's cinches have to be tight so that when a bronc rider launches himself onto his horse, the momentum won't take both of them and his saddle over the side. Not only is it embarrassing, but it's dangerous.

Pick up men also are used during bull riding. But they don't pluck the rider from the bull's back. They are there to "escort" a wayward bull back to the pen, or to run safety interference between bullfighters, riders, and bulls.

"It's a lot of fun," reports Kyle Encinias, eighteen years old. "It's an adrenaline rush." Pick up men—they're all about safety with some fun thrown in.

Medical Personnel

The first and last person a downed rider wants to see is the medic. The first because that means the rider is injured, the last because . . . he's injured. All rodeo cowboys know that it's not a matter of if they'll get hurt, but when and how badly. Good medics can help reduce further injuries.

"We're on stand-by," says Rio Grande Estates Fire Department Captain C. J. Schwartz at a recent rodeo. "We're ready to stabilize, then transport if needed." Rodeo cowboys don't say too much, but they're always glad to see the medics nearby.

Considered rodeo's "Red Cross," the Justin Sportsmedicine Program's doctors have been attending to PBR and PRCA's cowboys since 1981. Over the years, they've treated more than six thousand rodeo-related injuries. Taping ankles, applying ice, stitching up chins, relocating shoulders, and much more happen behind the scenes at a rodeo. Founded by Mobile Sports Medicine System's Don Andrews and Dallas Cowboys Team Doctor J. Pat Evans, Justin Sportsmedicine travels to over 150 rodeos annually. The director of medical services, Dr. Tandy Freeman, knows many of the rodeo riders by name, and can list their injuries.

Fig. 3.5.
A confused cowboy discusses his score with one of the judges.
PHOTO BY AUTHOR.

Rodeo cowboys pay an entry fee to ride, so their first question is—when can they return to the arena? Dr. Freeman takes into account the mental toughness of these men and women while he explains the severity of the injury and the treatment recommended. Usually, the cowboy listens, but the craving for coin in his pocket is a strong temptation to get up and ride again. It's hard to hold the cowboy down.

Bull riding accounts for the highest percentage of rodeo injuries—49 percent bareback riding—23 percent, saddle bronc—16 percent, steer wrestling—8 percent, calf roping—3 percent, and team roping—1 percent. The rodeo clowns/bullfighters are the most often injured noncontestants and account for almost 10 percent of the injuries received.

Medical personnel—quiet heroes of the rodeo world.

Veterinarians

Most of the PRCA's ten thousand members have lived or worked around animals their entire lives, and they possess a high degree of respect and yes, love for the livestock. Men with an even deeper interest in animals are veterinarians, and hundreds of them compete in professional rodeo.

Anyone who attends a PRCA rodeo can be assured that the utmost care has been taken to prevent injury to animals and contestants. PRCA's guidelines include more than sixty rules dealing with the care and treatment of animals.

Veterinarians are also on call in case of animal injury during a rodeo. They are hired just like the medical personnel and many specialize in rodeo-related injuries.

Secretaries

A most important, behind the scenes job is that of rodeo secretary. Responsible for organizing what appears to be chaos, the secretary records the times, figures the payoff, and hands out that prized check to the winning cowboys at the end of the rodeo.

Arena Judges

These men, usually dressed in striped shirts on the arena floor and carrying a clipboard, are responsible for enforcing all the PRCA rules. In most events, one judge is stationed close to the chute, the other farther in the arena. While each judge tries to watch all the action, the back judge (closer to the chute) is more responsible for citing incidents closer to his range of vision (such as marking out or barrier infringement). In case of a tied score between two riders, his score decides the winner.

Becoming a professional judge involves extensive training in the skills needed to evaluate livestock. They are tested on that knowledge and on rodeo in general.

PRCA judges undergo constant training and evaluation to ensure their skills are sharp and that they are enforcing the rules.

The brunt of many announcer's or barrel man's jokes, the judge knows his job and is not dissuaded by audience suggestions for higher scores.

Timers

Timed events—barrel racing, calf roping, team roping, and steer wrestling—all must be timed, down to milliseconds. The timer keeps the official time of the events and sounds the buzzer after eight seconds have elapsed in roughstock rodeo.

Fig. 3.6.
The gateman at this roughstock rodeo waits for the cowboy to nod his head. If he is too quick to open the gate, it could result in a re-ride option or injury to personnel. Often the bullfighter (clown) steps in to help in the chute.
PHOTO BY AUTHOR.

Chute Bosses and Laborers

Men behind the chutes poke, prod, holler, and flap their arms at the livestock. Or they may be helping a cowboy mount his animal in the chute. Or they just may be the man gripping the rope ready to open that gate when the rider nods his head. These are the chute laborers, the men who make the rodeo go smoothly.

Chute bosses direct the horses and/or livestock. Which animal goes first, which pen holds what, as well as the organization of the pens when the stock reenters the holding pen is his responsibility. It's a job that when done right, looks easy.

Flankman

This chute laborer has a specialized job. He's in charge of placing the flank strap on the bull or bronc, which is not nearly as easy as it sounds. Equipped with a long hook, much like an elongated clothes hanger with a hook at one end (called the flank hook), he places the padded strap on the animal's back, then fishes under the belly for the other end using the hook. He then draws it toward him and connects the flank strap.

Knowledge of each individual animal is essential. Some bulls perform better with loose flankstraps, others need to be tight. At no time does this strap injure the animal. It's just a reminder that it's time to buck.

Entertainers

Rodeo entertainers perform between events. Their entertainment, reminiscent of vaudeville acts, may take the form of daring rope tricks on horseback, dogs or monkeys on horses, trick riding, or clowns in crazy cars. Their job is to keep the excitement high and the pace quick.

In spite of their costumes and hilarious antics, clown barrel men during bull riding events are not rodeo entertainers. While they may have moments of mirth by joking with arena officials or the audience, their primary job is the safety of the rider and other clowns. (for more on barrel men, see the Clown chapter)

Rodeo Queens

These young women are the ambassadors of rodeo. They often lead the parade and wave and smile at the audience. Accomplished horsewomen themselves, they must possess a wide knowledge of rodeo as well as be available to represent rodeo at various functions. They usually reign for one year, and during that time wear the crown and sash with honor.

Here's a few of the questions these rodeo queens must be able to answer:

How many events are sanctioned by the PRCA?
Where is the National Finals Rodeo held?

Fig. 3.7.
Entertainers, such as this one at the Working Ranch Cowboy Rodeo Finals, provide laughs between rodeo events. Rope and horse tricks have been around over one hundred years. PHOTO BY MYKE GROVES.

Name a PRCA rodeo contractor from your state.

Name the twelve circuits of the PRCA.

What is the maximum number of points awarded in a roughstock event?

Name the horse that was chosen Bareback Horse of the Year last year.

What is the difference between WPRA and PWRA?

Define a legal catch in steer wrestling.

How many can you answer?

Rodeo arena personnel: the guys who make it happen. Our cowboy hats are off to you.

Fig. 4.1.
Bronc riding is an everyday chore on the ranch. Cowboys come to ranch
rodeos to demonstrate their riding expertise.
Photo by Bert Entwistle.

4

Ranch Rodeos: The Real Deal

Ranch rodeo gives ranch cowboys a chance
to compete and show their skills. It's a team sport.
—Gary Morton, former president, Working Ranch Cowboys Association

E VER MILK A COW? How about a one-thousand-pound cantankerous wild
cow who violently objects? Ever chase a four-hundred-pound calf that needs
branding . . . or doctoring . . . on horseback? Me, neither—but cowboys do.

Description

Today's ranches, much like those of yesteryear, require powerful working horses and
tough cowboys working as a team to wrangle unruly cattle through sagebrush, sand-
storms, and blizzards. And just as they did way back when, ranch hands brand, rope,
doctor, cut (sort), and herd cattle to trucks on their way to the market. The cowboy's
job in this twenty-first century is just as hard and just as important as it was over a
century and a half ago. And cowboys still enjoy letting off a little steam in friendly
competition between other ranches. For all their hard work, everyone takes home a
few bumps and bruises, but the winners also take home bragging rights.

Ranches raise cows, steers, calves, bulls, and horses. All of these critters need tend-
ing, and rugged, weathered cowboys have the distinct pleasure, day in and day out, of
putting their rears into saddles and heading into the rangeland to tend the stock.

Cowboys, while generally quiet and unassuming, enjoy an occasional sparring
event with other ranches. Who's the best bronc rider, or which team of ranch hands

can pen those yearlings the quickest? All they need are good horses and a friendly throwing down of the gauntlet.

Ranch rodeos give teams of cowboys a chance to show off their skill and teamwork in front of hundreds, perhaps thousands, of people. There are several events in this rodeo: bronc riding, team penning, team doctoring, wild cow milking, and team branding are standard, but rodeos may also include double mugging, trailer loading, and wild horse racing. Not every rodeo showcases all of these events, but at least four must be executed during a rodeo sanctioned by the Working Ranch Cowboys Association, and each event comes directly off the ranch and involves real working cowboys.

All events are timed, but in addition, others may be limited by the number of rope or loop throws. It may seem easy to lasso a calf and give it a hardy dose of medicine, but just watch any cowboy try to do it—it isn't a trot in the park. Cowboys spend hours each day in the saddle and most would rather conduct all their business from that perch. Hadley Barrett, WRCA announcer, likes to joke about a cowboy's inability to do anything on his feet. "They're about half worthless on foot when that right boot hits the ground and the left slides out of the stirrup." Ranch rodeos—nothing personal, it's just family.

Ranch rodeos are structured to demonstrate the skills of a working ranch cowboy. They also strive to preserve rural values, despite urbanization, and to throw a spotlight on today's ranching and cattle industry.

History

Ranch rodeo echoes the everyday duties and necessary teamwork associated with running a ranch. In the early years, many professional cowboys who started in ranch or community rodeos, such as the famous Miller Brothers 101 Ranch Wild West, were paid performers. Rodeos became more organized, offering prizes and prize money. In the 1930s and 1940s, the sport entered the professional world with organizers, entry fees, and even livestock contractors. Cowboys specialized in one or two events. Unfortunately, the cowboys who did the real work on a real ranch were pushed to one side.

However, the ranch rodeo is making a comeback, thanks in part to television coverage of the challenging and exciting grass-roots spectacle—rodeo.

In the 1980s and 1990s, cattlemen's associations and large ranches all across the West sponsored competitions between ranch cowhands. Each ranch provided a team of three to six cowboys to compete in these rodeos. But it wasn't until 1994, according to a WRCA historian, that a group of "visionaries" decided it was time to "bring the cowboy back to America" and gathered to form the Working Ranch Cowboys Association (WRCA). They assembled in Amarillo, Texas, and by March of 1995 had laid the groundwork of an association.

Their tenets are simple:

Preserve the heritage and lifestyle of the working ranch cowboy.
Promote ranching on the national level.
Organize and produce a World Championship Ranch Rodeo.
Assist cowboys in times of need through the scholarship and crisis fund.

Ranch rodeo is one of the fastest growing team sports in America today. Teams from all over the United States and Canada compete at local WRCA-sanctioned events, which earn them the opportunity to compete in the championship.

Who Competes?

A working ranch rodeo requires the contestants to be actual cowboys who make their living from a ranch. The working ranch must have at least a three-hundred-head cow/calf operation or run at least five hundred yearlings for minimally six months of the

Fig. 4.2.
Ranch bronc riding allows the competitor to hold on to anything while riding—just like on the range.
PHOTO BY BERT ENTWISTLE.

year. Day workers are allowed under certain conditions. A team is made up of four to six cowboys and may include women and teens as young as sixteen.

Ranch Bronc Riding

All ranches need an adequate supply of horses for working cattle, but no horse is born tame. It falls to the capable hands of a ranch cowboy to "start" these horses to become saddle broke, willing to let a human on its back. "No horse wants to be ridden," states National Finals Rodeo announcer Butch Knowles. But, ridden they are. And needed they are.

Bronc riding is the only portion of the ranch rodeo that is not a team effort. Only one team member competes. For this event, a brush bronc or stock pony, provided by a stock contractor, is ridden for eight seconds. The cowboy rides in what is called a "ride as ride can" style. "The way they ride them at home," says Barrett; which means hold on for dear life to anything and everything that keeps the rider off the ground. It is permissible to grab the saddle horn, touch the horse, use two hands on

Fig. 4.3.
One of the most entertaining events in ranch rodeo is wild cow milking. It takes four men to corral Bessie.
Photo by Bert Entwistle.

the rein (double grabbing), or hang on to the mane. "If the W on your Wranglers is higher than your ears, you're in trouble." Thanks again to Hadley Barrett.

Unlike "regular rodeo," this bronc riding event allows anything the cowboy can do to stay in the saddle. This may include keeping his free hand down (unlike the PRCA where the hand needs to be up). Barrett claims this hand-down technique is a "way to avoid walking a long way home." Cowboys don't like being parted from their saddles.

Similar to a traditional rodeo, pick up men ride in the arena to help the cowboy either by giving him a hand off the bronc or chasing down the animal once the rider has dismounted. Also, a strap is secured to the horse's flank, which serves only to remind the animal to buck.

The contestant must use a regular stock saddle; no PRCA rigging is allowed. They may not hobble one or both stirrups. "Hobbling the stirrups would be to tie them together underneath the horse's belly or to the cinch in some way to keep the saddle on," explains WRCA board member Edna Mae Holden. The horse must be saddled for everyday use. A regular bucking horse halter with one rein must be used and is provided by the ranch team. Points, which count toward a team's standing, are awarded for the difficulty of the horse as well as the degree of aggressiveness and control demonstrated by the rider. A re-ride (opportunity for another ride on a different horse) may be awarded at the judge's discretion.

So, just what does the bronc rider win? Five thousand dollars at the world championship and tons of bragging rights.

Wild Cow Milking

This event sounds as riotous as it really is. On the ranch, a cow that's lost her calf needs milking down or an orphaned calf may need milk. Cowboys corral the cow and then milk her. She's just as uncooperative on the range as she is in the arena.

In this timed event, a wild cow is turned out in the arena or cut out from a herd. All four team members are involved in this challenge, but only one, the roper, is on horseback. After the cow is roped, the rest of the team does whatever it takes to stop that animal. They grab the tail, clutch her around the neck, plant their heels in the dirt (oftentimes the rest of their body, too), and try to bring her to a standstill long enough to get milk into the quarter-sized opening of a longneck bottle. Once that's accomplished, it's still not over. A runner, possibly the milker or another team member, must run to the finish line—which is usually a circle at the end of the arena—and hand the bottle to a judge, who pours out the milk—any amount of milk will do. Meanwhile, the rest of the team works to get that rope off the cow's neck as the clock won't stop running until that's done, too.

Wild cow milking is one of the more dangerous events in a ranch rodeo: pasture cattle tend to have sharp horns and hooves, and a cranky disposition, unlike the

Fig. 4.4.
Once the milk is collected in a tall-neck bottle, the cowboy must run to a
circle and pour out the milk. The flag is lowered when he reaches that circle.
Photo by Myke Groves.

docile dairy cattle. The Charolais cows will even head butt the roper's horse. None
of the cows like being touched except by their own small suckling calf. Even on good
days, they can be hard to handle. Because they are mature cows, these animals are
also the biggest cattle used in any of the events. Think twelve hundred to two thousand pounds or a VW Bug.

Scoring and rules are simple. When the cow clears the gate leaving the alley, a
flag is dropped by the back judge, and the clock starts. There is a two-minute time
limit as well as a two-loop limit to rope the cow. The cow's head must pass through
the loop and the cowboy's rope must be off the saddle horn before milking starts.
The roper dismounts and helps with the mugging (wrestling the cow to a standstill)
or milking. Any team member may milk the cow. If no milk is collected, or the milk
will not pour out, the team receives a "No Time," which translates to no points. The
team with the fastest time wins.

In addition to time, points are counted toward the final team tally. WRCA
Championship arena record for wild cow milking is 20.76 seconds by the Chain
Land & Cattle Company.

Team Penning

One of the most popular events in ranch rodeo is team penning—truly a team sport. It requires the cowboys to read and judge the cattle's behavior. Three cows or calves must be separated from a herd of as many as thirty. Patience, teamwork, and good cutting horses will win every time. Team members must keep the three cattle apart from the rest of the herd and drive them into a pen at the other end of the arena. Winner is determined by the fastest time.

In this three-minute timed event, as the riders approach the starting line, the announcer will call out a number, and at that point the team must cross the line and begin cutting (sorting out and separating) the designated three cows. Only one rider is allowed in the herd at a time. The other two cowboys push and separate the stock and nudge the proper ones toward a sixteen-foot square portable pen, which has an opening facing the herd. Since cattle have that "herd mentality," it's even more difficult to get them into a pen when they'd much rather be shoulder to shoulder with other cows. Once the three correct animals are penned, at least one rider must

Fig. 4.5.
This ranch team must cut out three predesignated calves, then herd them across the arena and into a holding pen.
PHOTO BY MYKE GROVES.

enter with them and raise his hands. The clock stops at that point. The team with the fastest time wins. Points are awarded to the team.

The rules are straightforward. Three correctly identified cows are guided into the pen. More than one man in the herd adds a thirty-second penalty. The team may call for time with only two cows. No more than five cows may cross the line while cutting is taking place or the team receives a "no time." There is a thirty-second penalty for loping into the herd. Unnecessary roughness of the cattle, decided by the judge, disqualifies the team. Also, the riders can't contact the cattle with hands, hats, ropes, bats, or any other equipment. Other than that, it's easy.

Team penning requires not only skill and a good horse, but also teamwork and the understanding by each member of just what his job entails. Each cutter (cowboy) has specific jobs to do, but communication with each other is paramount.

The first cutter sets the pace and the tone of the event. He must let his partners know which way he's entering the herd, either verbally or by hand signal, then bring out the first cow quickly. He drops off the cow and returns as fast as possible (without loping or startling the herd) to act as turn back for the original turn back rider (cutter no. 3). The turn back rider is the one who is in charge of keeping the nondesignated cattle corralled or turned back, in one part of the arena.

Cutter number 2 heads left to compact the herd assuming the first cutter has gone right. A good number 2 rider doesn't get out of the herd until he's clear. He isolates his cow while the number 1 rider is getting clear, which means he's ready to cut when the turn back gets there. The number 2 cutter keeps an eye out for the rest of the designated cattle and helps by calling to his partner. Turn backs do the same thing. This helps everyone do his job and shaves seconds off the time.

All cowboys know to give the cattle space. "Sometimes, the best thing you can do is slow down when working cattle," states Barrett. So a team member may hang back a little (checking the horse) and let the cow relax. If that cow thinks he's not "the one," chances are he'll be more cooperative. Once that cow is cut, the cowboy pushes him along the fence toward that pen. If all goes well, the cow will enter the enclosure or at least stand near it waiting for the others to join. If the cows do not enter the pen, the cowboys nudge them toward the entrance, keeping their horses between them and the rest of the herd. Cows will often make a break for the safety of the others.

All different breeds of cattle are used for this ranch rodeo event. Many cowboys agree that it's not the breed that makes a difference in the cattle's performance, but their background. Did they come off a large ranch or a feed lot? Are they part of a large herd or small? And the weather can be a major factor. Animals sense a change in weather and it manifests itself in their behavior. An approaching storm causes unrest.

WRCA championship arena record for team penning is 38.10 seconds by H. Cross Cattle Company in 1998.

Team Branding

A brand is a mark, usually burned, into an animal's hide that denotes the owner. Since the small calves tend to look alike, this system makes identification easy. Announcer Barrett states, "Fences and brands make good neighbors."

On ranches, branding is performed after calving season in the spring. The brand is applied to the calf's hip or ribs with a hot iron. Freeze branding, marking with a dry-ice material, is moderately successful, but generally is not allowed to be registered with state agencies. (For more on brands and branding, see Glossary).

During the ranch rodeo, the calves are not branded with hot irons, but rather with chalk. There are no fires or hot instruments of any kind used during the rodeo. Other than that, the rest of the event parallels the actions of cowboys on the range. The basis of team branding is that two cowboys ride into the herd, rope two calves with the same designated number, and bring them to the other two cowboys. There, the calves are "branded" and released. The team with the fastest time wins.

Team branding requires four to six cowboys: a roper, two flankers, a brander, and two herd holders. Members from other teams may help out if the competing

Fig. 4.6.
In ranch rodeo, branding is done with a bucket of chalk,
but it still takes cowboy teamwork to get the job done.
PHOTO BY BERT ENTWISTLE.

team doesn't have enough hands. A herd of cows and calves are held behind a herd (chalk) line at the end of the arena. Time begins when the roper, who may only walk or trot his horse, heads into the herd to select the predesignated numbered calves. There is a two-minute time limit for this selection but no loop restrictions.

The calf is usually roped around the neck, but double hocking (both feet roped) or around the body is permissible. One leg roping then dragging is not allowed and results in disqualification. The cowboy drags the calf across the line where the flankers grab the animal and place it flat on its side. The rope is removed before the branding iron is taken out of the bucket of chalk. The ground crew has to be quick and keep an eye on the herd so that the other animals don't try to sneak across the line.

As soon as the rope is free from the calf, the roper returns to the herd. If there are two ropers, one will still be in the herd where he is looking for another calf, holding the herd, or ready to rope the next calf.

Once the calf is flat, the brander, using a chalk-covered branding iron, marks one side of the calf's ribs, then replaces the iron. Time stops when the iron is in the bucket after the last calf. A flag judge positioned near the bucket determines this.

Rules state that a calf must have returned to the herd before being roped again. If the roper enters the herd or drags the calf out at a lope, a thirty-second penalty is assessed. Also, the calf must not be jerked off its feet when it hits the end of the rope. If it does, a No-Time results.

The record arena time at the WRCA Championships in Amarillo is 33.94 seconds by the Wilson Cattle Co. & Ward Ranch in 2001.

Team Doctoring

Cattle are people, too—they get sick or hurt. And, just like people, they need some tender, lovin' care sometimes. Oftentimes, the cattle range is too remote for a regular veterinarian's visit. So it falls into the capable laps of the ranch hands to take care of the doctoring of cattle, anywhere from newly born calves to great big bulls. What these cowboys do on the range is identify the animal in question, separate it from the others, treat it, mark the animal's head, then release it. A few days later, they may go back and check on the animal's progress and then they may do more doctoring, or change the medicine.

In the ranch rodeo, the procedure is essentially the same, but the cowboys have only two minutes to get all that done. Three team members (header, heeler, "vet") enter the arena on horseback where a herd of yearlings, who weigh 350 to 550 pounds, wait at the other end. As the team approaches the start line, the announcer will call a number corresponding to a yearling. Time begins when the riders cross the start line. They must walk or trot into the herd (loping tends to frighten and scatter the herd when other animals may need doctoring); the designated yearling is cut from the herd and driven across the start line. The tricky part here is to keep the rest of the animals from accompanying the marked yearling (that good old herd mentality, again). No more than two cows are allowed to follow.

At this point, the rider, allowed up to three loops, ropes the yearling and the catch must be around the horns, head, half head, or head with one front leg. If the steer is caught by one horn, the roper may not ride up and place the rope over the other horn or head. While one rider is roping the head, another is roping the legs (the heeler). The heeler must rope one or both back legs, no front legs. The vet, who has been allowed to hold the cattle, dismounts once the header and heeler face each other, as in traditional steer roping, and he's then ready to mug the steer and administer the "medicine."

Once the yearling is caught, the other two riders must then dismount and lay the unwilling critter on its side with all four legs visible. At this point, the vet will place a chalk mark between the animal's eyes, usually a line drawn down the fore-head. Failure to do this results in a No-Time. Head ropes must be removed before the vet raises his arms once the line is drawn, to stop the clock.

Fig. 4.7.
Doctoring on the ranch is usually done by the cowboys where they tag the animal with a "chalk" grease marker to identify which animal has been tended. Note the "chalk" line on the calf's head.
Photo by Bert Entwistle.

The chalk mark is not chalk at all, but colored clay grease paint sticks, much like fat crayons. The paint, available in a rainbow of colors, is impervious to rain, snow, and sweat. One official states that with "a lot of soap and water and scrubbing, it may come off." And he's talking about the cowboy's hands.

The team with the shortest time wins and is awarded points, which count toward the team's total. WRCA arena record for team doctoring is 16.99 seconds by Turkey Track Ranch in 2000.

According to Martin Black, nationally recognized ranch horse and cattle dog trainer, a single cowboy who needs to doctor the cattle will do it all from the saddle. He eases the horse up to the cow, plants a foot on the cow's head, then leans over and applies the medicine, or injection. He then marks the cow. All is done with economy of motion in mind. Black says, "Don't get off your horse unless you have to." Spoken like a true cowboy.

Rules

Strict rules govern all WRCA rodeo contestants. Long pants and long-sleeved shirts must be worn in the arena, along with cowboy boots and a cowboy hat. Chaps and spurs should be worn in all events except Wild Cow Milking and the Wild Horse Race. Animal abuse is prohibited as is loud, obnoxious profanity or unsportsmanlike conduct.

Rodeos

Ranch rodeos are held around the country and Canada throughout the year. Mac & Pat Scott's Ranch Rodeo in New Cambridge, Missouri, is the only ranch rodeo in the country that is held in a pasture with no arena fences to contain the cattle. The historic Guitar Ranch (founded 1906) in Abilene, Texas, sponsors the Western Heritage Classic Ranch Rodeo. The Colorado Championship Ranch Rodeo is held in Hugo, Colorado, every summer. The Working Ranch Cowboys Rodeo Championship is held in Amarillo, Texas, in November.

Check the Internet for local information.

Associations

American Quarter Horse Association
Colorado Cattlemen's Association
National Team Penning Championships
Ranch Horse Association of America
United States Team Roping Championships
Working Ranch Cowboys Association

Rodeo doesn't get much wilder than a typical ranch rodeo. But it's all in fun, with a bit of bragging thrown in. "It's not about winning," says Burr Gagan, Oklahoma's Adcock

Ranch team captain, "it's about competing and having fun. Ranch rodeo is a family deal. It's not a one person deal. Other ranches help out."

WRCA president Gary Morton says, "Watching the interaction, and the good horses work in the various events, is great."

Cowboy Hall of Fame rodeo announcer Hadley Barrett summed up ranch rodeos and the cowboy way of life. "Cowboys support each other, and the only boundaries are the sky and the river."

Fig. 5.1.
Bull riding gets the heart and adrenaline
pumping for both rider and spectator.
PHOTO BY MYKE GROVES.

5

Bull Riding:
Not for the Faint of Heart

It's a strange sport . . . you sort of live life fully—you live on the edge.
—Mike Lee, 2004 PBR World Champion Bull Rider

66**T**HE WORLD'S MOST DANGEROUS SPORT." What an appropriate moniker to
pin on this exhilarating event. Where else would a 150-pound man strap
himself onto the back of an untamed 2000-pound animal? An animal that many
times would just as soon run over the man on his back after bucking him off.
Ah, bull riding!

History

Newest of the rodeo sports, bull riding has caught on like wildfire. Canada, Mexico,
Brazil, and Australia promote bull riding and send some of their finest cowboys to
the United States. Attended by more than twenty-five million spectators each year,
bull riding is also watched on nationally televised programs by over ninety million
people annually. And the numbers are growing.

Just what do people find so mesmerizing about bull riding? Could it be the
inherent danger, man versus beast? Does this sport hearken back to gladiator days,
stirring the blood?

Description

A rider first swings his body over the chute rail behind the "box," where the bull
stands, and settles on the bull's hips in front of the flank strap (for more, see

Glossary). Hanging his legs on either side of the bull's body may be difficult. A large bull takes up most of the room in the box and at times they lean against a rail, making it impossible for the cowboy to drop his leg into the proper position. In these cases other riders will push the bull with their feet, or in extreme cases, a two-by-four is used to wedge the bull over.

The rider, sitting in the middle of the bull's back, adjusts his bull rope. He does this by finding the fat pad between the bull's shoulder blades and placing his handle in this area. He then runs his hand up and down the rope that he has recently coated with a sticky resin (see Glossary). This allows him a firmer grip on the bull rope.

Slipping his hand into the handle, the rider brings the bull rope over his hand and under his wrist, thus strapping his hand into the pad. Another rider pulls the rope tail upward, which tightens the strap under the bull's chest.

The cowboy's hand is now firmly wedged between the bull's fat pad and the handle. A quick pull of the rope tail, however, will release his hand.

Fig. 5.2.
This bull and rider have just exited the chute, where the bull turned right.
Note the fringe on the rider's chaps giving more movement to the ride.
Photo by Myke Groves.

The rider "scoots up" on the bull rope and positions his rear on the upper center of the bull's back. The handle, which he pulls up on, is gripped near the cowboy's groin. His knees clench the bull's sides and his toes are turned out. The rider squares his chest with the bull's head and shoulders and focuses on the bull's head. Only when the rider feels he is positioned well, and that the bull is ready to go, will the cowboy nod his head.

At this signal, the gateman flings open the gate and the timing starts. The clock starts ticking when the bull's head leaves the chute gate.

During the ride, the cowboy must keep his hand in the bull rope and the other hand (the free hand) must not touch the bull in any way. Touching causes automatic disqualification. Riders position their free hands to their sides and hold up their arm in a "waving to the queen" action. This provides balance for the rider.

Spurring helps increase the score but is not imperative (unlike bronc riding) in order to receive a score. Bull spurs with blunted rowels will not hurt the bull in any way; they are designed to encourage the bull to buck as well as allow the rider to grip the sides better.

At the end of eight seconds, a buzzer sounds and the rider releases the tail of the rope, throws his leg over the bull's shoulder, and both feet hit the ground, thus resulting in a "get-off." At this point, the rider is able to make a quick getaway from the bull. Ideally, the rider and bull are headed in opposite directions.

A left-handed rider pulls the end or tail of his bull rope to loosen it, thus releasing his hand, then kicks his right leg over the bull's head. This will set him on the ground facing away from the bull, allowing him to run in the opposite direction of the bull. Bulls are strong and quick, but the split-second timing for that bull to turn around is usually all the lead time a cowboy needs for a successful getaway.

A right-handed rider performs the same drill in the get-off except he uses his left leg to swing over. Many times the bull will not cooperate and results in the cowboy plowing into the dirt.

The rider's job at the point of hitting the ground, whether on his feet or his rear, is to get away from the bull and to safety quickly. Not only is his life in danger but so are those of the cowboy protection team—the clowns. If at all possible, the rider rolls, crawls, or runs to the railing or behind the barrel until the bull is headed back to the holding pen.

Scoring: The Eight Seconds

Eight seconds. A short amount of time. Eight ticks of the second hand. A lifetime.

A bull rider must stay on the bull for a full eight seconds in order to qualify for points. The clock starts ticking when the bull's head leaves the chute gate.

Two judges tally points for each ride. They stand on opposite sides of the arena and each allows up to twenty-five points for the rider and twenty-five for the bull.

Fig. 5.3.
A good buck involves the bull's back legs extending up over the shoulders.
Photo by Myke Groves.

Added together, a total of one hundred points is possible. In professional riding, many times scores are over 90.

Judges are men who have ridden bulls themselves and are familiar with the sport as well as with the bulls. Bulls are judged by the height of the jumps, if they perform as expected. If the bull "flattens," doesn't lift his hind legs high enough, or performs below his norm, the score is lower.

The rider is automatically disqualified if, at any time, his free arm touches the bull before the buzzer, or if he leaves the bull's back before the eight seconds end.

Scores are lowered for the cowboy if he doesn't have control for the full eight seconds. This could include hanging on but sitting back on the bull's flanks or hanging on the side of the bull. While he may not touch the bull with his free hand or hit the ground, he still had no control. Some bulls don't buck as they're expected, or they come out of the chute gate wrong. The judges may award a re-ride if they feel a bull didn't give the cowboy the opportunity to score appropriately.

Riders choose to accept the re-ride. In some instances, the cowboy may feel that if he takes the re-ride he will have little or no chance of staying on, or if he is hurt he may decline the re-ride opportunity. Most other times, especially in the highly competitive professional world, riders will accept the re-ride, figuring any score is better than none, or their low scores are not competitive enough.

The perfect buck involves the rear end lifting higher than the bull's shoulders, then the front end lifting off the ground.

Belly rolls occur when the hind legs of the bull, in mid-jump, swing out right or left while the front legs remain on the ground. This causes the rider to lose balance and hit the ground before his eight seconds.

Leaving the gate, a bull may turn either right or left. Many bulls have a pattern they follow, and even though riders like to know what pattern the bull prefers, bulls are, after all, animals and very unpredictable.

The Riders

Bull riding is generally considered a young man's game, although an organization of "senior bull riders"—anyone over thirty-five—is growing in popularity. As most bull riders will admit, strength is important, but agility and mental stamina are the important components of a bull rider. While it may be a "young man's game," young women are finding a place in the bull-riding world as well. It's a rough sport. There is no way to get on the back of a one-ton bull, buck off, and not get hurt. "You can die or get hurt easily," states 2004 PBR World Champion Mike Lee.

A rider, male or female, must be eighteen to qualify for PRCA standings. Prior to that, riders climb up the ranks of junior rodeos, whether high school or collegiate.

Is there fear? Absolutely. "To me," says Ty Murray, seven-time world rodeo champion, "the essence of bull riding is it's so scary and there's so much adrenaline, that if you can stay focused and fluid through that and do your job right, that's a test like no other." Fear keeps a rider on the edge of his game . . . and spectators on the edge of their seats.

Famous Riders

Many great bull riders have ridden great bulls over the last hundred years. Lane Frost, Jim Shoulders, Charles Sampson, Ty Murray, and Chris Shivers stand out as exemplary riders. Each brought a style and attitude to the sport of bull riding that is incomparable.

Outstanding records have been set in the last few decades. Wade Leslie on the bull Wolfman scored a perfect 100 in Central Point, Oregon, in 1991. Denny Flynn won bragging rights with a 98 in 1979 and Don Gay rode for 97 points in 1977. Recently, Albuquerque's Michael Gaffney completed a ride for 96.5 points. Don Gay also has

Fig. 5.4.
Stretching, performed before every ride, helps reduce the
riders' injuries, such as pulled muscles and strained groin.
PHOTO BY HALEY CRAWFORD.

accumulated eight world titles and Jim Shoulders earned six consecutive titles from 1954 to 1959.

What is the allure of bull riding? Is it the adrenaline rush or the money that can be made? Or both? In 2000, Chris Shivers took home over a million dollars in one day when he won the PBR World Championship.

Equipment

Bull riding requires a bull rope with pad, flank rope with bells, a Kevlar vest, one glove, chaps, and boots with appropriate spurs. Helmets are not required but a few riders, especially those with recent injuries, wear them. Children under sixteen are required to wear them when competing. Otherwise, the cowboy hat is considered appropriate head gear.

The vest. Before 1992, most riders did not wear any kind of protective gear. PBR cofounder Cody Lambert designed a vest that is comprised of wide stays that run vertically and completely around the body, reminiscent of the nineteenth-century corsets. Velcro tabs at the shoulders and front allow the vest to adjust to fit the rider

Fig. 5.5. Mandatory equipment for bull riders includes a rope, vest, gloves (one), and many opt for a helmet or face protection. Photo by Haley Crawford.

snugly or to be ripped from the rider by the bull's horns. The Kevlar vest helps protect against horn jabs as well as displacing the weight of a bull's hooves. This vest has been credited with drastically reducing the number of serious chest and internal injuries among riders.

Mouthpiece. All riders wear a plastic athletic mouthpiece. This helps prevent broken teeth but also keeps the cowboy from biting down on his lip or tongue during the rough ride.

Helmets. Specially made bull-riding helmets, football helmets, or other athletic headgear may be worn to help protect against the most common injury—concussions. Bull-riding helmets consist of three wires that wrap in front of the face. There is a space of three-quarters of an inch between the wires, which does not allow the one-inch horns to penetrate. Rodeo safety rules require bull's horns to be cut no less than one inch in diameter.

Chaps. Made of leather, chaps cover the legs of the riders thus protecting the pants and skin beneath. Chaps were invented to protect the cowboy's legs against

Fig. 5.6.
Behind the chutes, cowboys fasten their chaps over sturdy, loose-fitting jeans. Chaps help protect legs from injury or scrapes.
PHOTO BY
HALEY CRAWFORD.

prickly bushes and the thorns of vegetation out on the range. Available in all sizes, as well as custom made, they wrap around the front and sides of the legs and hook in the inner thigh.

For rodeo purposes, in particular bull riding, chaps are made of slick leather designed so that a bull's horn will slide off the leather. The fringe on the edge creates visual excitement.

Spurs. The spurs' purpose is to help the rider hold on to the bull's sides and also encourage the bull to jump higher. Worn by all cowboys, spurs consist of metal straps that fit snugly around the boot heel and are tied down under the heel with twisted wire. Rowels, the rounded attachments that stick out from the back of the spurs, are blunted and held with wire to keep them stationary. The bull's thick hide is not injured.

Leather straps holding the metal spurs onto the boots are left with the tail ends flapping, which lessens the chance of getting the cowboy's foot caught in any loop. See the Glossary for a brief history of spurs.

Bull Rope. The bull rope consists of several feet of finely woven hemp or poly-styrene rope that wraps under the bull's chest. The pad with a handle slides over the rope to adjust to each bull's chest size. A portion of the rope is coated with resin that allows the rider's hand to better stick to the rope.

Many ropes are custom made. Riders decide if they prefer a thicker rope or thin-ner, whichever gives a better degree of control.

Gloves. Deer or calf skin gloves are worn on riding hands only. The free hand is uncovered. Riders tape their riding wrist with athletic tape in order to increase their hand's stability and to reduce injury.

Clothing

Bull riders wear long-sleeved western-styled shirts, loose-fitting jeans, and com-fortable boots. The pants should give enough room for the rider to move easily and breathe well. Shirts are fitted but not tight. Riders need room to move.

The Bulls

Bucking bulls are not taught or forced to buck. It is a trait bred into them. However, not every bull will buck. Due to increased and sophisticated breeding programs, genetics is the most prevalent factor in determining a bull's ability and desire to buck. A bull will only buck if he possesses the innate desire and instinct to do so.

Anyone who watches bull riding even once will hear the term *rank bull*. On the outset that may bring visions of stinky, aging bulls who can barely stand. However, in rodeo speak, a rank bull is the toughest of the tough. This bull bucks off most of the riders, may be unpredictable and even dangerous.

Fig. 5.7.
Bulls will contort their bodies any which way to dislodge the rider.
Note the bull bells hanging under his belly. In addition to making
noise, these help keep the bull rope under the belly.
PHOTO BY MYKE GROVES.

To achieve the status of "rank," a bull must have proven himself in the chute
and arena. For bulls, their buck-off statistics are just as important as the stay-on
statistics of the riders.

The legendary bull Bodacious, owned by Sammy Andrews, easily considered
the rankest of the rank, allowed only eight qualified rides in his many years in the
arena. Each ride scored in the 90s.

Bodacious consistently jumped high out of the chute. Since the bull jumped
higher than the top bar on the chute, when he came down to kick, he'd kick well
above the chute. "Bo's first jump when he left the chute resembled a roller coaster
ride," says Andrews's wife, Caroline. Most riders were unseated on that first jump.

"Bodacious could roll and kick, and he learned how to unseat a rider. Bo really
liked to get in the air. And, every time he jumped, he usually brought a bull rider

forward." When a bull drops and jumps straight up again quickly, the chances of a head-to-head collision are great. With the bull rider flying forward, Bo's head would come back and collide with the rider. This resulted in horrendous wrecks. Tuff Hedeman, former president of the PBR, spent months recovering from head and chest injuries resulting from such a collision with Bodacious.

Due to his bucking style, however, Bodacious eventually proved so dangerous to riders that his owners retired him to pasture and stud farm until his untimely death by kidney failure in 1999.

Other rank bulls include Red Rock, whose record speaks for itself—one ride out of three hundred. Lane Frost, who died in Cheyenne, Wyoming, after a bull-riding accident, performed that one ride.

Legendary rank bull Dillinger, voted the 2000 PBR Bucking Bull of the Year, retired in 2002 due to a leg injury. Also legendary are Little Yellow Jacket, the 2001, 2003, and 2004 PBR Bucking Bull; and Red Wolf, who retired in 2000 at age thirteen and now lives on a Texas ranch where he is enjoying his time in the breeding program.

The Stock Contractors

Stock contractors own and tend the bulls. Chad Herrington, the 2000 Stock Contractor of the Year; Nevada Berger; H. D. Page; Casper Baca; and many others all pay big bucks to take good care of their bulls.

These contractors provide the best bulls in the world for rodeos throughout the United States. A contractor trucks in bulls to the rodeo and is responsible for their care. Because of the high value of these animals, the bulls are given quality grain and hay and attended by a veterinarian regularly. Bulls are bucked carefully as bucking too often strains their muscles. Many of the contractors try to keep the same feeding schedule and routine for the bulls while on the road.

So You Want to Be a Bull Rider?

Many bull riders grow up on ranches or with rodeo families, and therefore are around bulls since childhood. However, a few successful cowboys didn't begin to ride until their early twenties. Men and women of all ages ride bulls. But because bull riding is so physically tough, it's not for everyone.

The best way to learn the art of bull riding is to attend a bull-riding school. It is usually a three-day school instructed by nationally ranked bull riders. The best schools conduct bullfighting (clowns) instruction in tandem with bull-riding lessons. Larry Lancaster in Denver runs such a school, as does Lyle Sankey in California, and Terry Don West in Oklahoma.

Visit the Internet under Bull Riding Schools for up-to-date information and requirements. Participants must be in good health. Each school stresses the fact that as a novice, if the student feels at any time bull riding is not for them, he or she

Fig. 5.8.
Author not making a successful (or graceful) ride out of the chute.
A bull-riding school is a great place to learn the mechanics. Note Hall
of Fame inductee Charles Sampson (in white hat) in the background.
PHOTO BY MYKE GROVES.

is free to sit out. At no time is a student forced to ride. This sport is too dangerous to insist that everyone try it. As five-time world champion bullfighter Rob Smets states, "There's no dishonor in not riding. Bull riding's not for everyone."

Riders may start as young as three on sheep. These tykes are called "wool riders." They graduate up to steers as preteens. By early teen years, riders may ride young bulls. By eighteen, they may ride mature bulls.

After attending bull-riding schools, it is highly recommended to find a practice pen and work at the craft of bull riding daily.

How Dangerous Is Bull Riding—Really?

Bull riding is billed as the "World's Most Dangerous Sport" for good reason. Consider this: a 150-pound man will ride a 2,000-pound muscle machine for eight seconds.

The bull's goal is to get this person off its back and return to the pen where food and friends await.

The most common injury is a concussion, according to Dr. Tandy Freeman, director of medical services for the Professional Bull Riders' Justin Sportsmedicine Team. These head injuries range anywhere from headache inducing to life threatening. Such an injury often occurs either when the rider's head comes in contact with the bull's head or horn, or the rider hits his head after being thrown from the bull.

Helmets help reduce the impact, but certainly do not eliminate the threat. Many riders feel that helmets restrict their peripheral vision and are too constricting.

Another common injury is pulled groin muscles, where the thigh meets the lower abdomen. Riders warm up by stretching before riding, which helps reduce muscle injury.

Shoulder injuries, to either arm, is the most common surgically treated injury, according to Dr. Freeman. An estimated 12 percent of all surgical procedures that PBR contestants undergo are for shoulder damage.

Bull riding: definitely not for everyone. "Bull riders are different," Dr. Tandy Freeman states. "You've got to be different to get on a bull. There is a certain degree of toughness and mental fortitude that all bull riders share. Those are not necessarily common traits in every professional sport."

"It's such a neat, and awesome, and intimidating feeling all at once," reports Ty Murray, "it makes the hair on the back of your neck stand up."

Associations

Professional Rodeo Cowboys Association (PRCA)
Professional Bull Riders (PBR)
All Pro Bull Riders
Canadian Pro Bull Riders
Major League Bull Riding
Professional Senior Bull Riders (PSBR)
Professional Women's Rodeo Association (roughstock affiliate of Women's
        Professional Rodeo Association)
Southern Pro Bull Riders

Fig. 6.1.
One bullfighter climbs out of the barrel to aid the cowboy and his partner.
Photo by Myke Groves.

6

Send in the Clowns:
The Cowboy Protection Team

My greatest satisfaction is saving the riders, helping them out of a tight spot.
—Dennis Johnson, PBR five-time finals qualifier bullfighter

Clowns. Everybody loves the clowns. Real clowns make people laugh, but for these rodeo clowns, the bullfighters, there's nothing funny about their job. They protect the cowboy.

The Cowboy Protection Team is commonly referred to as bullfighters. In the United States, bulls are not "fought" by matadors with capes. No bull is killed for sport. No bullfighter in the United States stands in front of an enraged bull and attempts to match wits with it. Our bullfighters match wits with bulls that will come out of the chute again next week—very alive, very ready to buck off anyone brave enough to climb on their backs.

Rodeo clowns have been around almost as long as rodeo itself. But it wasn't until the late 1920s, with the introduction of the aggressive Brahma bull, that rodeo clowning took on a more serious nature. Brahma bulls are known to attack downed riders, so bull-fighting clowns became a genuine necessity.

The job of bullfighters is critical—they must engage the bull and lure him away as the rider scrambles to safety.

Inside the rodeo arena, timing is everything. Timing is critical not just for the rider trying to stay on the two-thousand-pound bull, but also for those trying to avoid being hooked or trampled by one.

The world of the rodeo bullfighter is one where a fraction of a second can mean the difference between a bruise and a serious injury. Even with skill and technique, the most experienced bullfighters are not without their share of bruises, torn ligaments, and broken bones.

Under that Greasepaint Are Life Savers—Bullfighters

Despite the facade of colorful shirts, baggy pants, and face paint, the bullfighter is all work, his attention riveted on his job. A bullfighter's tactic is to distract the bull when a rider either bucks off or dismounts after his ride. Distraction provided by the bullfighter gives the rider a chance to get back on his feet and out of harm's way.

The bullfighter relies on his athletic prowess, precision timing, and ability to think on his feet. He makes decisions in milliseconds that could mean life or death for either himself or the bull rider, whose life has been placed in his hands. Armed only with inner courage, bullfighters carry no ropes or weapons. Instead, they possess a willingness to face death with a defiance that is incomparable in any sport.

There is no room for mistakes.

The traits required of a good bullfighter include speed, agility, and a sense of the bucking bull's instincts.

What's Inside that Barrel? A Barrel Man

Although dressed similarly to the bullfighters, the barrel man's job differs from the bullfighters. A barrel man's duty is to entertain the crowd during the "down time" that is inherent when working with animals. When bulls are being loaded or not cooperating in the chutes or during breaks in the action, a barrel man takes over and jokes with the audience and/or the announcer.

But that's not his only job. The other is much more serious. His heavy, custom-made "walking" barrel placed in the arena's center serves as protection against rampaging bulls. A rider finds safety behind the barrel in case he is bucked off far from the arena fence or bucking chutes.

Techniques—Protective

Bullfighters do not create action, they anticipate action and then react. They position themselves advantageously. The bullfighters work as a team to maintain protective coverage for the bull riders to escape. This teamwork is crucial. They must react to each other's moves to maintain a parallel position on either side of the bull at all times. One wrong move or misread cue could spell disaster for both the bull riders and bullfighters.

Situated on each side of the chute when the bull turns out, the bullfighters wait for the action. The bull dictates where the bullfighters will be at all times during the

Fig. 6.2.
Two bullfighters step in to save the fallen cowboy.
PHOTO BY MYKE GROVES.

ride. They must be able to react instinctively to the bull's actions and to be able to give the rider every possible opportunity to escape uninjured.

The bullfighters analyze not only every move the bull makes, but the rider as well. In so doing, the bullfighters can prevent a wreck by spotting little things that the rider or bull is doing. In fact, according to bullfighter Dennis Johnson, they give certain hand signals to each other indicating what could happen. For example, a hand between a little finger means the cowboy has taken a "suicide wrap," which is one way a rider positions his hand in the bull rope. Another signal indicates that this particular bull is meaner than others. A "heads up."

Sometimes there is nothing the team can do to prevent an injury or wreck, but they can distract the bull long enough to assist the rider.

When a rider gets hung up in the bull rope or his spurs get caught in a flank strap, the clowns work as a team to get him free. One bullfighter will go to the bull's head to get the bull's attention while the second bullfighter will go to the rider's hand and work to get him untangled.

Jim McLain, head coordinator for the Professional Bullfighters Tour, said, "Bullfighting requires agility, speed, finesse and what bullfighters like to refer to as

Fig. 6.3.
The bullfighter's main duty is to distract the bull so that the rider can get away unharmed.
PHOTO BY MYKE GROVES.

'bull savvy'—instinctively reading and anticipating the bull's moves. Bulls are not dumb," McLain says. "They're very intelligent, they have their own personality and distinct way of doing things."

McLain states that when the bullfighter engages a bull, it becomes a precision sport where every move counts.

Techniques—Freestyle

Very different from protective bullfighting, freestyle is the ultimate solo engagement of man and beast. The beast is the fighting bull, unlike the bucking bull. Mexican fighting bulls, which are smaller than bucking bulls, are inherently angry, athletic, and ill tempered.

While not a part of the rodeo's timed events, freestyle bullfighting has become a real treat for spectators. In this event, the bullfighter engages the bull for a minimum of forty seconds with an additional thirty seconds optional.

The objective of freestyle bullfighting is to engage the bull with maneuvers that put the bullfighter directly in the danger zone for as long as possible without losing control. He must read the bull and decide how to fight. The freestyle bullfighter can create the action with the bull, based on the bull's aggressiveness.

In an interview with *ProBullrider* magazine, five-time World Champion Bullfighter Rob Smets explained. "It's a one-on-one, 70-second freestyle competition in which the bullfighter will be judged according to the skill he displays in maneuvering the animal. The goal of the bullfighter is to control the animal versus being controlled by the animal. Points are awarded accordingly, based upon how well the athlete maneuvers the 2,000-pound bull. Precision in jumping the bull and handling the barrel, as well as contact with the bull, are also credit-earning situations."

With the freestyle bullfighting competition growing in popularity, this unique event is featured at the Cheyenne Frontier Days as well as during the PBR Finals in Las Vegas.

Equipment and Clothing

In addition to agility and good reflexes, the rodeo bullfighter must possess a vest similar to the Kevlar vest that the riders use, and knee and elbow pads. Their baggy outfits are deceptively designed so that in case of an encounter with the bull's horns, the clothes tear away from the bullfighter's body, thus enabling the man to escape.

Fig. 6.4.
Baggy clothes
provide room for
bullfighter Chris
Burke to maneuver.
Underneath is
a protective vest.
PHOTO BY
MYKE GROVES.

As more and more corporations are discovering bull riding, many are willing to sponsor and promote this fascinating, exhilarating sport. The bullfighters may wear clothes that aren't so "clownish" and are embellished with corporate sponsor logos.

So You Like to Clown Around? How to Become One

Bullfighting school, according to several professional bullfighters, is the best way to learn the basic protecting techniques. Schools are offered throughout the country, but potential students need to ask themselves several questions.

Why do I want to become a bullfighter? What's the real reason for wanting to plant myself in front of a one-ton beast?

The adrenaline rush as well as the danger factor certainly figure into the answer as do the love of the sport and respect for the cowboys.

Will I have time to work somewhere else? Many professional clowns work steady weekday jobs then rodeo on weekends close to home. A few do nothing but rodeo.

What do I know about bulls?

A good understanding of the animals helps considerably when anticipating a bull's moves.

If the student's knowledge is limited, many practice pens will allow people to work with the bulls. Attending rodeos is another way to learn, although behind-the-chute action is limited.

What would I do if I got hurt?

In the bull-riding/ bull-fighting arena, the question is never if, it's simply a matter of when and how much.

Those questions taken into account, a bull-fighting school is usually held in tandem with bull-riding schools. Most of these schools last three days, some as long as five, and are held in various states.

As with attending any school, especially one in which lives are at stake, ask questions of past participants and research the instructors. Be sure they're highly experienced. The school may be expensive, but a high-quality school is well worth it.

Once the school is over, find a practice pen and practice. The bullfighter's life as well as that of his partner and rider is on the line, so experience is the best teacher.

It is highly recommended that a bullfighter not hire on at a rodeo until he has quite a bit of experience as a protective bullfighter. And talk about job stress, the bullfighter's quick reflexes and thinking mean the difference between life and death.

"It takes a long while to learn," states Dennis Johnson. "There's a lot to learn."

How Dangerous Is Being a Bullfighter?

As in any rodeo sport, injuries will happen. It's certainly not a question of if, but only how often and how badly. Injuries to rodeo noncontestants are highest among the bullfighters. The reason is obvious. They throw themselves in front of a ton of

Fig. 6.5.
Could you step in front of a one-ton animal? Bullfighters come in close contact over one hundred times each weekend. PHOTO BY MYKE GROVES.

moving animal. Broken bones, concussions, bruises, and ankle sprains are common. In fact, 10 percent of rodeo injuries involve the bullfighters.

Fortunately, medical personnel are always on hand at every PRCA- and PBR-sanctioned event. In case of injury, the bullfighters know that they will be in capable hands.

Associations

Midwest Bullfighters Association
National Federation of Professional Bullriders
Rodeo Clowns and Bullfighters Association

Bullfighters. Their passion for the sport and their willingness to come between man and beast is thrilling. These men have been referred to as a cross between incredibly crazy and extraordinarily brave. Whichever they are, they are the true heroes of the rodeo world.

Fig. 7.1.
A classic rodeo event, saddle bronc riding
comes directly off necessary ranch duties.
PHOTO BY MYKE GROVES.

Saddle Bronc Riding:
Rodeo's Classic Event

Being in the classic event, it's pretty neat.
It's easier on your body than other roughstock.
—Billy Etbauer, 2004 WNFR World Champion Saddle Bronc Rider

SADDLE BRONC RIDING IS THE CORNERSTONE OF RODEO. The classic event. This hair-raising, spine-jarring, breathtaking whirl of horse and cowboy is one-third of all roughstock events. Roughstock refers to just that—horses and bulls that are not tamed, therefore *rough*. All animals will buck, but the better equine athletes are bred to increase the animals' natural ability. Nowadays, careful records are kept, and new genetic engineering is available to help ensure good bucking stock. In no way are horses and bulls taught to buck. Can't be done. Instead, they are encouraged to do what comes naturally.

History
Saddle bronc riding comes directly off the range, its history rooted deep in man's need for transportation—something other than his own two feet. Early on, man discovered that riding a horse was faster, and in many ways easier, than using his own energy, so taming that four-legged mode of transportation became necessary. And in the American West, where vast plains give way to more plains or tall mountains, a durable form of long-range transport was paramount. The ranches raised hundreds and thousands heads of cattle that tended to roam over those vast expanses. The cowboy in charge of those herds relied on his horse to get his job done.

In order to get a working horse to work, ranch hands had to catch and gentle a horse, then halter and saddle it. That was the easy part. Once they were mounted, the cowboy would ride the horse until it "gentled" enough to accept a rider. This process was not fast or easy, but necessary. Many cowboys picked themselves up off the dirt countless times until that bronc understood who was boss.

Things haven't changed. Horses still start life wild and unwilling to have someone on their back. They still must be gentled.

While horses' natures haven't changed, neither have the cowboys'. There's that competitive spirit in all of them. Naturally, way back when, they got together to prove who was the better saddle bronc rider. Who could fight that bronc down to a standstill? Who had the best style? Who could stay on the longest? Good-natured competitions grew into organized contests, which grew into rodeo. Saddle bronc riding, it is claimed, was the first rodeo event in the first "official" rodeo in Deer Trail, Colorado, back in 1869.

And saddle bronc riding was just bronc riding in rodeos until the 1920s, because there was no bareback riding and *everyone* knew that bronc riding was with a saddle.

Fig. 7.2.
Lined up like soldiers, these horses wait their turn to put cowboys in the dirt.
PHOTO BY AUTHOR.

Fig. 7.3.
Preparing to ride, this cowboy is assisted by other riders
and chute personnel. Mental focusing is a must.
PHOTO BY AUTHOR.

Description

A saddled bronc stands in the chute, or box, at the end of an arena. The box is large enough for the horse to comfortably stand but not big enough for the horse to maneuver much. Iron pipes are used to form the box. A flank strap (see Glossary) has been placed around his middle and a saddle secured before the rider gets into the box. Once the bronc is placed in the chute, a cowboy or cowgirl eases down from on top of the horse and sits. The cowboy sticks his boot heels into thin stirrups, grips a thick halter rope with one hand, leans back into his specially made saddle, and positions both of his feet over the bronc's shoulder. This is to give the horse the advantage.

Once the rider feels ready, he nods his head, the chute gate swings open, and both cowboy and horse explode into the arena. The horse leaps and bucks, the rider rakes his spurs from the shoulder back toward the flanks—this action is called a mark out. The idea is to stay synchronized with the horse's movement. The rider must constantly lift on the hack rein to keep his seat in the saddle while his free arm is held away from his body and the horse.

"Watch for the cowboy's movement of feet," says 2004 WNFR World Champion Saddle Bronc Rider Billy Etbauer. "They should be in the horse's neck before the (horse's) front feet hit the ground." Pure poetry in motion. A fluid ride.

In this event, rhythm is the key. And spurring is the way to get it. Model spurring begins with the rider's feet far forward on the horse's point of shoulder, then once the horse has completed his first jump out of the chute, he sweeps his feet back toward the cantle, the back part of the saddle seat, as the horse bucks. The rider then snaps his feet forward toward the horse's neck a split second before the animal's front feet hit the ground. He does this for the entire eight seconds.

Not only does the cowboy have to swing his legs from the bronc's shoulder to his flank; he also must hold onto a thick and braided halter rein. He must adjust his grip to maintain balance and avoid being pulled over the front end or launched out of the saddle. His riding hand and rein must be on the same side.

Fig. 7.4.
This cowboy is doing everything he can to make the eight seconds. Note the pick up man on the other side.
Photo by Myke Groves.

At the end of eight seconds, the buzzer sounds and usually two pick up men are right there to assist the cowboy. One may ride alongside to offer a helping hand while the other speeds after the bronc to release the flank strap and head it into the holding pen. Often, the pick up men ride between the horse and cowboy, allowing the rider a second or two to rush to safety.

Scoring

All it takes is eight seconds in the saddle. However, many other factors are figured into a saddle bronc rider's score. A rider who synchronizes his spurring with the animal's bucking receives a high score as well as demonstrating control throughout his entire ride. The length of the spurring strokes, reaching the full length of the arc with toes turned outward, and how hard the horse bucks, impact the 100-point-possible score. Toes are turned outward thus allowing more spur contact with the horse. As in all roughstock events, the two judges each award up to 25 points for the animal and up to 25 points for the rider. A perfect score would be 100. A score in the high 80s is considered good.

The bronc itself is rated on how high he kicks, the strength and force of the bucking action, direction reversals, and for his rolling and twisting action.

Disqualification results if during the ride the cowboy touches the animal, himself, or his equipment with his free hand. It gets harder. If either foot slips out of the stirrup, if he drops the halter rein or changes to the other hand, or if he fails to have his feet in the proper "mark out" position prior to the ride, he receives a no-score. Of course, if he's bucked off before the eight scores, all he gets are bruises.

Rodeo spectators ooh and aah over the wild rides, but with saddle bronc riding, a wild, uncontrolled ride is scored much lower than a "tame" one. Saddle bronc riding often appears effortless, but it's only because of the cowboy's skill and hours of practice.

Equipment and Clothing

Equipment used is a saddle, head collar, and a single rein, or (hack) halter rein, which must be held with one hand. The saddles, which average fifteen hundred dollars, are lightweight and have no saddle horn like the traditional roping saddles. The stirrup leathers are farther forward than usual and the cantle, skirt part of the seat, is higher than traditional saddles. The pommel, or the front part, is higher than traditional. In addition, cowboys use a long thick rein, known as the hack rein, attached to the halter on the horse's head.

Flank straps are used in bucking events to encourage a horse to kick higher. The strap must be lined with fleece or neoprene and placed loosely around the horse's flank area. To pull it tightly would cause the animal to stop, which is not desired. Horse flank straps are equipped with a quick release mechanism that allows the pick up men to release the strap when the ride is over.

Cowboys at PRCA-sanctioned rodeos wear long-sleeved shirts, jeans, cowboy hats, chaps, and spurs. The spurs are blunt-roweled and are not locked. They roll along the horse's skin. Riders are disqualified if their spurs are too sharp or if the animal is injured in any way due to the rider's actions. The protective Kevlar vests are worn to help prevent internal injuries such as cracked ribs.

Injuries

The most common injury for saddle bronc riders is getting thrown over the front of the horse and being stepped on. The result is lacerations, bruises, and possible concussion. Ankle and shoulder injury as well as broken collarbones are common also.

While saddle bronc riding is dangerous, as is any rodeo sport, it is particularly injury laden. According to a study done by the Justin Sportsmedicine Team, of all the

Fig. 7.5.
Chute personnel pull the rider out of the chute, out of harm's way, when the horse decides not to cooperate.
Photo by Myke Groves.

rodeo injuries in a ten-year period, 15.5 percent were during saddle bronc riding. Of course bull riding topped the chart at 49 percent.

Famous Riders

Casey Tibbs, possibly the most famous rodeo athlete of all time, is best known for his saddle bronc riding. He is the only rodeo contestant ever to win the saddle bronc and bareback riding championships in the same year (1951). A native of South Dakota, Tibbs won six saddle bronc riding titles, two all-around titles, and a bareback riding championship between 1949 and 1959. A twenty-foot bronze statue of Tibbs sits outside the ProRodeo Hall of Fame in Colorado Springs, Colorado. He sits astride the famed saddle bronc Necktie.

Tom Three Persons of the Canadian Blood Reserve was the first Indian world champion saddle bronc rider. In 1912, at the age of twenty-six, he entered the first few days of the first Calgary Stampede, and did reasonably well. The final day, he drew Cyclone, said to be unrideable (he'd thrown the previous 129 riders). His trick was to rear wildly, balancing on his hind legs, then thud to the ground with a bone-jarring whump. In those days, there was no eight-second limit, you just rode until you came off or the horse stopped bucking. Three Persons rode Cyclone to a standstill. The crowd went wild. As new world champion, he won one thousand dollars, a medal, a handmade trophy saddle, a championship belt, and a gold and silver mounted buckle. Three Persons was the first contestant to be inducted into the Canadian Cowboy Hall of Fame.

Women won many events through the 1930s. Bonnie McCarrol won the 1922 Women's Saddle Bronc Riding title at the Frontier Days, and Lorena Tricky won the Ladies' Saddle Bronc Riding title in 1921.

More recently, Oklahoman Billy Etbauer has won five world titles since 1992 in addition to his sixteen NFR qualifications. In 2003, Etbauer set a Wrangler NFR arena record with a 93-point ride and won the fifth round.

Horses

How do they make them buck? As mentioned earlier, it's part of their nature. But in the rodeo world, they use horses that have a greater inclination to buck. The origination of rodeo bucking stock is the 40 percent that have continued to buck off their owners and riders. They come from the racetrack, feed lots, ranches, and just about everywhere else there are horses. These are considered too dangerous for other equine activities, yet they are perfect for bareback and saddle bronc riding. Stock contractors constantly receive calls from owners who cannot train their animals to stop bucking.

The other way horses make it into professional rodeo is breeding. They are bred with other fine, proven buckers. Almost opposite from thoroughbred race horses who are bred to have the "buck" taken out, saddle bronc horses are bred to have the "buck" stronger than ever.

Two types of bucking horses are used in rodeos, one for saddle bronc and the other bareback. Bareback horses tend to be smaller with a wilder bucking style while saddle broncs are generally larger with a more "classic" style of bucking. This allows the rider to sit up in the saddle and get a rhythm with his feet forward. Many saddle horses are draft-horse crosses. These large sturdy animals have the perfect bucking action combined with durability and strength—excellent attributes for long-term rodeo careers.

One indicator of the suitability of horses to rodeo is their longevity of life and career. For example, High Tide, a legendary bucking horse, bucked off a nineteen-year-old cowboy at the National Finals. High Tide was thirty-two. It is not unusual for a horse to be in his mid-twenties and still put cowboys on their pockets every time out of the chute.

Fig. 7.6.
A good warm-up with stretching and envisioning a successful ride
helps the cowboys hear that buzzer while still on the horse.
PHOTO BY AUTHOR.

How to Become a Saddle Bronc Rider

So you want to be a saddle bronc rider? Billy Etbauer admits that "it takes a lot of horses to learn." But he also encourages people to "go out and do it. You just gotta get on a lot of them [horses]." Many cowboys claim that saddle bronc riding is the toughest rodeo event to master because of the technical skills necessary to learn.

One good way to learn is by attending a bronc riding school. There are several around the United States, but before attending, be sure to check with other students and professionals. Sankey Rodeo Schools explain and practice the correct dismount, perfect bucking chute techniques, and safety concepts. Ten time WNFR qualifier Dan Etbauer runs saddle bronc riding schools around the country. Check the Internet for more information. Most schools get students on the stock the first day, but only after excellent preparation.

Associations

International Professional Rodeo Association
Professional Rodeo Cowboys Association
Professional Women's Rodeo Association (roughstock affiliate of Women's Professional Rodeo Association)

Saddle bronc riding—it's kind of like two-stepping with a four-legged partner. The choreography of style and grace distinguish this event and these riders from all the others. It's truly the classic event of rodeo.

Fig. 8.1.
Bareback riding is hard on the body, but is pure poetry in motion.
Photo by Haley Crawford.

8

Bareback Riding:
Who Needs a Saddle?

Bareback riding, when it's done right, feels like you're floating on air.
—Kelly Timberman, 2004 WNFR World Champion Bareback Rider

FLOATING ON AIR? Is Timberman crazy? What about the brute strength it takes to stay on? Or the spine-jarring gyrations of the crow hoppers (broncs who do nothing but spring up and down like thousand-pound kangaroos)? How about that it's a bareback rider's job to look graceful while on the demented end of a pogo stick? Sure he's crazy, but not for a bareback rider. Timberman admits there's nothing else as exciting as riding those wild horses.

History

Bareback riding got a late start in the world of rodeo events. Up through the 1920s, with few exceptions, all bronc riding included a saddle, because that was the way cowboys rode stock on the range. After all, rodeo was just a showy extension of ranch chores. During the 1912 Calgary Stampede, bareback riding was introduced when a cowboy used just a rope around the bronc to hold on to.

While bareback riding is touted as a "newcomer," in truth when man first discovered that he could use this four-legged animal as a means of transportation, did he have a saddle? No. It's not even a case of which came first—the horse or the saddle. So bareback riders hold their heads up with pride, for they know *theirs* was the original rodeo event if there ever was one.

Description

Usually the first event to start off a rodeo, bareback riding is wild, unpredictable, and exhilarating. And that's just from the spectator's point of view. Bareback riding in its simplest form is a person seating himself on the back of an untamed horse and holding on to nothing but a suitcase handle for eight seconds. When the whistle blows, the rider gets off, hopefully into the arms of a pick up man. The cowboy waves his hat and walks away.

In its more complex form, bareback riding is the toughest, roughest, most nerve-jarring event in rodeo. "Twice as physical as football and wrestling combined," states Timberman.

Behind the chute, the cowboys get ready for their eight seconds of glory. About an hour before the ride, they stretch (probably the most important way for them to keep healthy), tighten their spurs, resin their gloves, and tell jokes. Michael Vigil, former Colorado bareback rider, states that joking and nervous laughter among cowboys before the event is part of the game: "There's no cowboy back there who

Fig. 8.2.
Stretching before any exercise is a great idea. Leg stretching helps reduce pulled groin muscles.
PHOTO BY
HALEY CRAWFORD.

isn't nervous." Riding is the ultimate adrenaline rush, but every person who rides knows the inherent danger of the sport.

Most bareback riders wrap their riding arms from well above the elbow to almost the wrist with elastic bandages. They crook the elbow in a ninety-degree angle so that during the ride when the horse jerks down, the cowboy's combined brute strength and wrapping help him stay on top. If the rider's arm straightens out, the muscles aren't strong enough to keep him upright on that bronc, and when he flies off that horse he has a good chance of tearing arm muscles.

Bucking spurs on the heel of his boots, neck collar in place, hat firmly pulled down over his forehead, the bronc rider slips his own rigging onto the back of the horse standing in the chute. It takes at least two people to get the surcingle, or girdle-like band, under the horse's belly. One fishes under the horse using a hooked wire to catch the end of the strap, while the other man tries to keep the horse calm and the rigging on the animal. Once it's tightened, the rider then adjusts his rigging, closely resembling a flat leather pancake with a suitcase handle in the middle, on the bronc's back. Each cowboy provides his own rigging.

The thick leather handle is just large enough for a rider to get his gloved hand into. Using resin, the rider coats both glove and handle to allow a firmer grip. Vigil points out that riders who use too much resin run the risk of having their hand sticking during dismount. He's seen cowboys who are hung up, unable to extract their hand, come off the side of the horse, and like a ragdoll, drag alongside. Chances of getting stepped on at this point are good.

When it's his turn, the rider positions himself above the bronc that is corralled in a tight iron-railed chute, and lowers himself onto that horse. He slides his gloved hand, palm up, into the handle, then grips it with everything he's got. With that done, he leans far back over the horse's back, positions his heels above the horse's shoulders, raises his free hand, and nods his head. The chute gate swings open and the cowboy's world blurs into a frenzy.

"The adrenaline rush is always there," says Vigil. Behind the chutes, other riders, officials, and stock contractors yell and holler, encouraging a good ride. All the noise and excitement keep that energy flowing.

The bronc bucks, and now it's grace and rhythm that will win the cowboy his gold buckle. After the initial jump from the chute, the rider pulls his knees up, dragging his spurs along the horse's shoulders and ends up toward the flank. When the horse's head comes down, the rider straightens his legs in anticipation of the next buck. At this point, the cowboy leans back so as not to somersault over the horse's head and end up beneath his hooves.

When the bronc comes up, the rider strengthens his grip on the handle, and positions his body as close to it as he can. His feet should be back under him. A good ride happens when the cowboy captures the horse's rhythm. This harmonious

Fig. 8.3.
Rodeo is truly
a group effort.
Cowboys, chute
personnel, and
other riders help out
behind the chutes.
Photo by
Myke Groves.

melding of animal and man creates a feeling of floating on air, like a bird flying. "It's an elite feeling," states Timberman.

After eight seconds, the buzzer sounds and it's time to get off. Two pick up men wedge the bronc between them, and in an ideal situation, the rider slides his hand out of the handle and launches himself into the waiting arms of the closest pick up man. Once most of the rider's body is off the wild bronc, the pick up man will rein his horse away from the bronc and drop the rider to the ground, preferably on his feet. At this point, the rider keeps a close eye on that bronc and makes his way toward a gate. Meanwhile, the pick up men gallop at breakneck speed to pull off the bronc's flank strap, equipped with a quick-release mechanism, then nudge that animal toward the holding pen.

Scoring

As in all roughstock events, a total possible 100 points may be awarded. The two judges, one closest to the chute or the "back" judge, the other farther into the arena, assign up to 25 points per rider and horse each. They combine their scores, which for a good ride will hover in the high 80s. If riders' scores are tied, higher points from the back judge determine the winner.

To acquire a score, the cowboy must do several things. First, both spurs have to be touching the bronc's shoulders until the horse's feet hit the ground after the initial move from the chute. Called a "mark out" in both bareback and saddle bronc riding, a rider who fails to do this is disqualified. This is the first thing judges watch for.

Second, he must still be on board that pogo stick when the buzzer or whistle indicates eight seconds, or an eternity, have passed.

Third, he must keep his free arm away from his body, the horse, and/or his equipment. Touching any one of these gives him a no-score. After the buzzer, the rider will use both hands to grip the handle and extract his sticky hand. That is perfectly okay.

Fig. 8.4.
Talking to your horse and letting him "get to know you,"
helps increase the rider's chance of making the eight seconds.
PHOTO BY AUTHOR.

Fourth, to put points in his pocket, he's demonstrated he's had control and kept hold of the rigging during the ride. If his hand slips out, more than likely he'll end up on the ground. Scoring is based on the horse and the rider. A cowboy earns higher points based on his spurring technique (the higher and wilder the better), the degree to which his toes are turned out while he's spurring. He's got to be willing to take whatever might come during his ride—his "exposure" to the horse's strength. Grace under fire, so to speak.

The bronc scores are based on their power, speed, and agility. Their high-kicking action, how hard they buck, lunge, and hit the ground, changing direction, as well as degree of rolling and twisting, influence the points. The wilder the better.

Equipment and Clothing

Nothing says "cowboy" more than a hat, chaps, and spurs. A bareback rider is all cowboy. In Professional Rodeo Cowboys Association–sanctioned events, a dress code is in effect for all contestants, male and female. Long-sleeved western-style shirts, buttoned at the wrist and tucked in, are mandatory. Western-style hats, jeans, and cowboy boots are required. Bucking spurs must have rowels (the circular metal part at the end of the spur) with rounded tips. This spur allows the rider to encourage the horse to buck, but will not in any way hurt the animal.

Chaps, leather leg coverings, are used to help protect the rider's legs when coming in contact with the fence or the ground. Added fringe gives the illusion of more action during the riding, so many cowboys opt for this design when buying chaps. Most bareback riders choose the long chaps, instead of the mid-calf style called "shorties" or "chinks."

Required equipment, compared to other rodeo events, is rather sparse. WNFR World Champion Kelly Timberman suggests not putting a limit on good equipment. "You must have faith in your equipment," he says; otherwise a cowboy could be worrying if his handle will break at just the wrong moment, instead of concentrating on making the best ride possible.

Bareback rigging, consisting of a wide rawhide strap with attached handle, ranges in cost anywhere from 350 dollars to 500 dollars. A formed bareback pad runs about 80 dollars. Bucking spurs with rowels average 45 dollars. The bareback vest with collar and neck brace run upwards of 250 dollars. The glove (you buy only one) is made of steerhide or deerskin with seams sewn outside, and may cost 30 to 40 dollars. Unlike regular clothing, roughstock gloves are purchased for either right or left hand, but not both. Equipment and clothing are available through feed and tack stores, western-wear stores, or on-line through special bareback-riding suppliers.

Fig. 8.5.
Chaps help protect the cowboy's legs from wayward hooves and dirt clods.
PHOTO BY HALEY CRAWFORD.

Injuries

Riding a stick-pony jackhammer with only one hand can be hard on a body. Bareback riding, too. Because of the power and speed of the horse, bareback riders suffer a tremendous amount of strain on their riding arm. Hyperextended elbows (imagine holding onto that suitcase handle and flying off sideways without letting go—ouch!), torn biceps, separated shoulders, and neck injuries are the more typical complaints associated with this extreme sport. Lower back pain, spinal damage, and tailbone injuries can occur, too.

Injuries can happen before the rider nods his head and leaps into the arena. Rider Michael Vigil remembers sitting in the chute and having a v-shaped chunk bitten out of his upper arm. He admits he may have spurred that bronc a little harder during the ride. In other cases, broncs, with cowboy attached, have tried to bolt over the chute's iron railing. Being sandwiched between iron and raging horse muscle can result in broken bones or at least bad bruises.

On the other hand, proper training, exercise, safety equipment, and preparation, such as stretching, as well as immediate medical treatment can prevent or at least lessen the injuries. Vigil recommends getting to know the horse before riding him. "Let him smell you, then he won't be afraid of you when you get on."

According to the Justin Sportsmedicine Team, of all the injuries received during a regular rodeo, 23 percent belong to bareback riders. Bull riders account for 49 percent while team ropers pride themselves on less than 1 percent of all rodeo injuries.

Horses

Bareback bucking horses tend to be smaller than saddle broncs, which means they're fast—real fast. To give a cowboy a good ride with high points attached, the bronc needs to be agile and a high kicker. The wilder the better.

As in saddle bronc horses, many barebacks come to rodeos because they buck. Owners, for whatever reason, need tamed horses and some animals refuse to yield. Fortunately for rodeo, these high-spirited horses often find themselves in arenas.

Classic Velvet is a good example. A registered quarter horse, he bucked too much to be used in team roping. Cotton Rosser, California stock contractor, bought him and turned the horse into a rodeo star. Classic Velvet bucked for seventeen years and was named the "Bareback Bucking Horse of the Year" in 1981. He retired at twenty-four, was inducted into the ProRodeo Hall of Fame in Colorado Springs, Colorado, and spent the rest of his days on a ranch nearby.

Other rodeo horses are bred and born to bucking stock herds. They come directly from ranches and stock contractors' herds.

Horses are not taught to buck, it's an inherent trait. Encouragement and incentives such as spurs and flank straps can help, but the horse ultimately will do what he wants. These animals are the lifeblood of stock contractors and the source of

Fig. 8.6.
Bareback bucking stock tends to be smaller and quicker than saddle bronc.
PHOTO BY HALEY CRAWFORD.

rodeo cowboys' livelihood. It's in the best interest of everyone involved to be sure these animals are well treated. *There are more rules (sixty-plus) governing the safety of livestock than for the cowboys themselves.*

Most horses grow to love the rodeo life. They get to remain wild and free, working only eight seconds a day, while their counterparts remain under control and the saddle for most of their career.

Famous Riders

Sixteen-time world champion Jim Shoulders is the first to spring to mind when the word *bareback* is mentioned. This professional rodeo legend has more world championships under his belt than any cowboy. Shoulders, the only professional cowboy to be honored in the Madison Square Garden Hall of Fame, was inducted into Oklahoma's Hall of Fame in 1975, and in 1989 to Oklahoma's Sports Hall of Fame.

Jim Shoulders won his first check to the tune of eighteen dollars at the age of fourteen, and from there was unstoppable. He turned professional the same year he graduated from high school in 1946. A short three years later, he catapulted to World Champion All-Around Cowboy. He went on to win five all-around, seven bull riding, and four bareback riding championships—bull riding and bareback titles the same year.

Now that he's retired, he raises bucking stock and runs the family ranch in Oklahoma. He has owned some of the most famous bucking stock in rodeo, including Andy Capp, Mighty Mouse, and Tornado (unridden for seven years). Tornado is buried at the Cowboy Hall of Fame in Oklahoma City.

Not surprising to country-music fans, singer/songwriter and 2005 ProRodeo Hall of Fame Inductee Chris LeDoux, who died in 2005, twice won Wyoming's bareback title while still in high school in Cheyenne. He went on with his music and riding and by 1976 won the Bareback Bronc World Title. LeDoux continued in rodeo until 1984, when he accumulated enough injuries to make him hang up his spurs. Fortunately, he didn't hang up his guitar. His songs reflect ranching and the rodeo life.

Marjorie Mae Roberts, called Margie, was a beautiful awe-inspiring woman who grew up to be a nationally acclaimed trick rider and champion bareback rider. Born in 1916, Margie grew up on horseback and gravitated to rodeo. Her family was known for putting on impromptu rodeos, and she was not to be left out. She originated the "diving girl" trick ride in which she stood in the saddle and leaned far forward over the neck of her speeding horse. She joined the Clyde Miller Wild West Show.

She rode bareback at all the big rodeos including Cheyenne and Madison Square Garden. In 1940, she won the women's bronc riding at the Cheyenne Frontier Days. Margie was inducted posthumously into the National Cowgirl Hall of Fame in Fort Worth, Texas, in 1987, five years after her death.

Hall of Fame induction would be great, but 2004 WNFR World Champion Bareback Rider Kelly Timberman would settle just to keep doing what he's doing—riding. "I love what I do—love to see the horses, the livestock. I feel most comfortable in rodeo."

Timberman should feel comfortable. He set a new single-season earnings record in bareback riding in 2004 with 225,000 dollars. Not bad for someone who just started competing six years ago.

One of his most memorable rides was on Classic Pro Rodeo's Dippin Wise Guy, who gave Timberman an 87-point ride. But he certainly won't forget winning the Star of Texas Rodeo in Austin in 2003, or the fact that in 2002 he was the Mountain States Circuit bareback riding champion. Yep, not bad for a beginner, an admitted "late bloomer."

So You Want to Be a Bareback Rider?

Timberman suggests "don't be afraid to follow your dreams. Stay focused. It takes lots of hard work."

Bareback riders are extremists. Anyone in the rodeo world knows that the combination of powerful animals and adrenaline-rushed cowboys is unparalleled. But they also know that the decision to become a rider must be taken seriously.

"It's not a spur of the moment decision," says Michael Vigil. "You'll get hurt if you just jump on." Get close to the animals, talk to people who ride, listen to their stories. Make informed decisions. Then, if you still want to try, have someone teach you the basics—what to do and not to do. Safety comes first.

The first time out, Vigil explains, the rider will see not much more than black. "That's the fear pumping inside you." If the rider survives that fear, he suggests getting on another bronc. With each progressive ride, the view gets better.

Rodeo schools, such as Sankey's, provide trained, skilled instructors who make the experience as safe as possible. Other bronc riding schools are located throughout the United States, Canada, and Australia.

After attending school or private lessons, it's a matter of practice, practice, practice.

Associations

> Australian Professional Rodeo Association
> Canadian Professional Cowboys Association
> Professional Rodeo Cowboys Association
> Professional Women's Rodeo Association (roughstock affiliate of the Women's
>   Professional Rodeo Association)

Bareback riding. This teeth-jarring, whiplash-inducing dance between man and animal exposes the essence of rodeo—rhythm and grace. Bareback riding.

"It's all good," says Kelly Timberman. "There's so much involved in it—being atop something that's so uncontrollable and being able to hang on to the whistle."

Fig. 9.1.
Steer wrestling, bulldogging, is a "big man's" sport.
It takes muscle and agility to wrestle a steer to the ground.
Photo by Bob Willis.

9

Steer Wrestling:
Taking the Doggie by the Horns

The best part of steer wrestling is just trying to make the best run you can with
the steer you've got, knowing you've accomplished what you set out to do.
—Luke Branquinho, 2004 WNFR World Champion Steer Wrestler

S TEER WRESTLING RAISES THE PHRASE "take the bull by the horns" to a new level.
While it's not exactly a grown bull these men grab by the horns, 550 pounds of
beef on four hooves is still mighty impressive. Why would a man pitch himself off a
perfectly good horse, running close to thirty miles per hour, just to jump on a loping steer that doesn't want to be touched much less thrown to the ground? The only
answer? Steer wrestlers are a breed all their own.

History
It's said that steer wrestling is the only rodeo sport that did not directly come out
of working-ranch chores. Rodeos evolved from cowboys strutting their prowess at
roping and bronc riding. But when do cowboys actually jump off a horse and wrestle
a steer to a standstill? It does happen, but it usually takes more than one man with
a rope to subdue the critter.

Formerly known as bulldogging (a steer is a "doggie"), this sport was invented by
Bill Pickett, an African-American cowboy. Pickett, back in the 1870s, had two cousins
who were trail drivers. He grew up listening to their exciting stories and dreaming of
the day that he too would be a cowboy.

One day, the story is told, Pickett watched cattle dogs controlling cattle by holding a cow's lower lip with its teeth. He thought he could do the same thing. Some weeks later, while passing a group of cowboys on his way home from school, he noticed they were having trouble branding their calves. He asked if he could help. He bit into the calf's lip after it was laid on the ground. This up-close-and-personal encounter—the first of many—worked. He held the calf while the cowboys branded it. By the time Pickett was fifteen, he'd worked as a cowhand on ranches throughout Texas and perfected his unique style of subduing cattle.

Bill Pickett and his brother Tom gave bulldogging exhibitions at the first Taylor (Texas) County Fair in 1888. After that he toured throughout Texas and by 1900 made out-of-state appearances as well. In 1905, back in Texas, Pickett, known as "The Dusky Demon," helped stage a Wild West Show in front of sixty-five thousand people. From 1907 to 1914, he toured with the show throughout the world—from delighted throngs at New York's Madison Square Garden to the king and queen of England.

In 1905, Pickett appeared in a Wild West Show at Madison Square Garden with the famed humorist and his friend Will Rogers riding beside him. Rogers's job (now known as a hazer) was to keep the steer heading in the right direction. At this particular time, the steer came out of the chute at a fast clip, ran toward the arena's fence, and jumped over. The audience panicked, of course, and tried to run away. Pickett and Rogers dismounted, ran after the steer, and caught it on the third balcony level. After Rogers cornered it, Pickett grabbed its horns and brought it back to the arena, much to the audience's relief. Thus, steer wrestling was born.

Bill Pickett died in 1932 and Zack Miller, owner of the Texas 101 Ranch, said of him, "Bill Pickett was the greatest sweat-and-dirt cowhand that ever lived—bar none."

Pickett, the first African-American to be inducted into the National Rodeo Cowboy Hall of Fame at Oklahoma City, was also inducted into the ProRodeo Hall of Fame at Colorado Springs. A bronze statue of him is displayed at the North Fort Worth Historical Society. The Bill Pickett Invitational Rodeo is the only touring African-American rodeo in the United States. Profits go to a fund for young, aspiring African-American cowboy athletes. And in 1994, the U.S. Postal Service issued a commemorative stamp in his honor. It was discovered, however, that the face on the stamp was that of his brother, Ben. All five million sheets of stamps were recalled. The U.S. Postal Service plans to reissue the corrected stamp soon—with Bill's picture this time.

Description

Steer wrestling is a timed event and the object is simple: Wrestle a 550-pound steer down to the ground. Not as easy as it might sound. That steer is fast, strong, and agile and it won't be "overpowered" by the bulldogger.

Fig. 9.2.
The steer is given a head start followed closely by the bulldogger and hazer.
PHOTO BY BOB WILLIS.

The cowboy waits on horseback in a fenced area, the *box*. A nylon rope barrier (see Glossary) is placed across the box and the steer is loaded into the roping chute. As soon as the cowboy nods his head, the steer is released. Then the steer, which has been given a head start, runs out of its own chute and past what is known as the advantage point. The contestant bolts out of the box and catches up to the steer's left side, the hazer on the right. By now, on an average run, they have covered 150 feet in less than four seconds.

When the wrestler's horse pulls even with the steer and his hip is even with the steer's hip, he slides off the right side of his horse (which is not the usual dismounting side), grabs for horns, and aims his pockets for the dirt. If he leans forward or back too far, he can lose his grip and end up under hooves. He needs his body to be upright. A seasoned bulldogging horse feels the rider ease off. At that moment, the

Fig. 9.3.
Bulldoggers plant their heels in the dirt as soon as they grasp
the steers horns. Kind of like stopping a sluggish freight train.
Photo by Bob Willis.

mount speeds up so the cowboy's feet slip easily out of the stirrups. The steer wrestler pulls free of his horse and digs his heels into the dirt, planting his feet in front of him. If the bulldogger is wearing spurs, at this point they roll up under his jeans and out of the way. They are not cinched under the heel in the style used by bull riders.

After the catch, the steer wrestler brings the doggie to a stop and/or changes the direction of the animal's body before the throw. His right elbow crooks around the steer's right horn and lifts up toward his left shoulder. He places his left hand under the steer's jaw and pushes down toward his left pocket, causing the nose to come up as if the steer and cowboy are about to share a kiss.

The steer by now starts to arc and slow down. The bulldogger cups the steer's nose in the crook of his arm and pulls in for another kiss. This forces the steer's head back and its body to fall. If the animal hits the ground fast and falls like it should, that's referred to as a "pancake."

The clock stops when the steer is on its side with all four legs aiming the same way. A winning time is usually between three to four seconds.

Luke Branquinho, 2004 WNFR World Champion Steer Wrestler, suggests that spectators "watch how the cowboy rides his horse. It makes a difference whether he wins or loses." He adds that "fast time generally wins the competition."

Scoring

The steer wrestler competes against other cowboys and the stopwatch. Timing begins when the bulldogger's horse breaks the barrier line at the front of the box. The clock stops when the steer is on its side with all four legs pointing in the same direction.

The bulldogger will add much time to the clock if he fails to bring the steer to a stop. And if he has to change the direction of the animal's body before the throw, it would be almost impossible to win. In addition, the contestant must give the steer a head start that trips an automatic barrier strung in front of the horse in the roping box. If the horse breaks through before the steer trips it, the contestant is given a ten-second penalty, which usually means he is out of the money.

If the bulldogger drops too far forward onto the head of the doggie and is knocked down (called a Houlihan), he must allow the steer to regain its feet. Then the cowboy throws it legally. If the steer falls to the opposite side than the wrestler is trying to throw it, or falls with one or more legs underneath its body (dog fall), the doggie's head must be straightened while keeping it on the ground, or the animal must be rethrown. A third miscue occurs when the steer plants its front feet well apart (rubber neck), requiring a full-nelson hold on the head. Not only do these add excitement to the sport, but time on the clock—which is not good if you're the steer wrestler.

Who Are the Bulldoggers?

Steer wrestling is known as the "big man's sport," and for good reason. The average weight for a bulldogger is 216 pounds and he stands 6'2". Just for comparison, a bull rider averages 161 pounds and measures 5'10".

These athletes possess strength, speed, and a sense of timing. In addition, they must understand the principles of leverage in order to take down a 550-pound steer. Timing and balance come into play as the bulldogger reaches the steer and slides down the side of his galloping horse.

Strength and dexterity are paramount qualities in a steer wrestler. Once the cowboy has hooked his right arm around the steer's horns, he extends his legs forward and plants his feet in the dirt, bringing the steer to a halt.

The hazer rides along the steer's right side to keep it running straight. He must keep the steer close to the bulldogger so that he can lean out of his saddle to grasp the steer's horns. His efforts are nearly as important as those of the steer wrestler. For that reason, oftentimes the bulldogger provides a horse for the hazer and gives him 25 percent of his winnings.

According to NFR qualifier Vernon Honeyfield, a hazer who is chosen by the bulldogger is usually a friend or relative but also someone known as a good rider with lots of experience. "It takes a unique rider—a very seasoned rider" to be a good hazer, he says.

Fig. 9.4.
A well-trained horse is vital for the cowboy to win. The hazer, the mounted cowboy, keeps the steer running close to the bulldogger. Hazers are invaluable.
Photo by Bob Willis.

Once that steer runs out of the chute and is past the advantage point, it's the hazer's job to ride just slightly faster than the steer. He "pushes" the animal as the cowboy eases out of his saddle ready to grasp those horns. And in the case where the steer avoids the bulldogger's first attempt, the hazer guides the steer next to the fence and heads it back toward the contestant for a second try.

Once the bulldogger has the steer in hand, the hazer continues riding past and watches the action. Many times he will secure the bulldogger's horse's reins and lead it out of the arena.

Equipment

A cowboy, a hazer, two horses, and a steer. Strong muscles, speed and timing. That's everything needed for steer wrestling. Since the wrestler uses only his hands to complete the task and his horse serves only as a form of transportation, no special equipment is required.

Famous Bulldoggers

Possibly the best-known steer wrestler is Bill Pickett, the father of bulldogging. He was the second child of thirteen from freed-slave parents. He married in 1890 and fathered nine children, the two boys dying in infancy, but all seven girls lived to adulthood. His unusual style of bringing a steer to its knees has never been duplicated.

Another famous bulldogger is Willard Combs, who was inducted into the National Cowboy and Western Heritage Hall of Fame.

Money can be made in bulldogging. Cash Myers won over 88,000 dollars in regular season in 2002 and over 176,000 dollars overall in 2001.

Homer Pettigrew won a total of six world titles for steer wrestling—1940, 1942–45, then 1948.

The fastest time in steer wrestling is 2.2 seconds by Oral Zumwalt in the 1930s; however, this was done without a barrier. In more modern events in which barriers are used, bulldoggers Jim Bynum, Todd Whatley (1955), then Gene Melton and Carl Deaton (1976) set the 2.4 seconds record time. With or without barriers, that's fast.

California cowboy Luke Branquinho has tucked one world title under his belt and looks forward to many more. In 1996, Branquinho won the California High School steer-wrestling championship, then in 1998 won the California High School all-around, steer wrestling, and team roping championships. He has qualified for the WNFR finals four times and already has won over 600,000 dollars. In 2004, he set the regular season earnings record (before the world finals) in steer wrestling with close to 126,000 dollars. Afterward, his single-season earnings record held at 194,000 dollars.

Injuries

Cowboys warm up before an event, just like any other athlete, but they do it bulldogger style. They stretch arms and legs then wrestle steers behind the chutes (known as "chute dogging") and even other cowboys who wander by too close.

Despite conditioning and stretching, the majority of bulldoggers' injuries are to their knees. The stress and strain of jamming their heels into dirt take their toll, resulting in blown-out knees. Even so, bulldoggers don't wear knee braces in the arena.

The margin of error is miniscule; the smallest mistake can lead to disaster. A steer stops and the cowboy misjudges the horn. It smacks the bulldogger in the middle of his face causing bruises, cuts, and/or a broken nose. Dislocated shoulders are not unusual. Less common injuries include taking a horn in the cowboy's belly when the steer's head isn't as close to the man's chest as it should be. World champion Rope Myers carries a two-inch scar in his abdomen. Hazers' shins reflect the colors of the rainbow. Eye punctures and even broken arms round out the list of possibilities. No protective gear, except that cowboy hat, long-sleeved shirt, jeans, and boots, are worn.

Fig. 9.5.
Bulldogging can take less time than it takes to yawn. Don't blink or you'll miss it.
PHOTO BY BOB WILLIS.

Injuries to the animals are few and far between. However, they occasionally suffer a broken horn, leg, or neck. This sport is a lot harder on the cowboy than the steer.

Steers

A steer differs from a bull in one very important way. Steers are castrated at an early age and bulls are not. Rodeo steers range in age from twelve to fifteen months, prime time for bulldogging. Their weight hovers around 550 pounds, while some breeds weigh a bit more. To qualify for this competition, steers must be at least 500 pounds and their horns must have a minimum length of eight inches from the base to the tip along the outside curvature of the horn. Steers are used in this event rather than calves because they are bigger and stronger and give the cowboys more of a challenge.

A preferred breed of stock for bulldogging as well as team roping is the Corriente steer. While most steers last in the rodeo world for a year, these can go two to three years. Their horns don't grow as fast as other breeds. And their endurance allows them to be roped repeatedly without fatigue and they withstand travel well. A good rodeo steer will be roped or wrestled many times in its career. Their easy temperament is important—they're not out to hurt the cowboy. They're known to come out of the chute fast and hard. Everything a bulldogger could want.

How to Become a Steer Wrestler

"If you want to be bulldogger," says Mavrick Parrish, former steer wrestler turned bull rider, "have your brother drive your truck at 35 miles per hour, then jump out and tackle a mailbox." Ouch.

Attending a steer wrestling school might be easier.

2001 WNFR Champion Steer Wrestler Rope Myers runs a steer wrestling school in Texas. In addition, younger brother Cash does, too. School information is available on line or through local tack and feed stores.

In order to win, 2004 WNFR Champion Luke Branquinho suggests a person "works hard. You gotta dedicate yourself, if you want to be good."

Associations

International Professional Rodeo Association
National High School Rodeo Association
National Intercollegiate Rodeo Association
Professional Rodeo Cowboys Association

Steer Wrestling. It's quick. A blink of an eye and it's all over. Of all the events in rodeo, it is said that steer wrestling offers the greatest amount of eye appeal to the spectator. It's a display of strength and an exhibition of finesse and skill. A true cowboy's sport.

Fig. 10.1.
Team ropers from New Mexico State University
Rodeo Team compete for national honors.
Photo by author.

10

Team Roping:
Two Men, Two Horses, and a Steer

The header is the quarterback, he starts the team, sets everything up.
—Speed Williams, 2004 WNFR World Champion Team Roping Header

The best part of being the heeler is not having to worry about
getting out of the chute. I let the header do the worrying.
—Rich Skelton, 2004 WNFR World Champion Team Roping Heeler

IMAGINE YOUR HORSE AT A DEAD STANDSTILL. A steer bolts out of the chute. You gig your horse in hot pursuit. Your partner spurs his horse and rushes into the arena. You rope that five-hundred-pound steer around the horns, then lead him to the left. Your teammate catches the steer's hind legs. That done, you both pull your ropes taut, and you turn your horse to face your partner. Team roping basics. World arena record is 3.5 seconds. Less time than it takes an average person to yawn.

History

Team roping is another rodeo event that comes directly off the range. Its roots run deep in everyday ranch work. Cattle must be caught in order to treat injuries, change brands due to transfer of ownership, or brand those who escaped branding as a calf. Cowboys learned that treating or branding these large, strong steers was too difficult—impossible most of the time—for one man alone. Therefore, they developed the system of team roping.

Out of necessity came rodeo's only true team event. But cowboys by nature are competitive, so somewhere at some time ranch hands turned team roping into a competition. By the early 1900s, team roping found a home in rodeo, but not officially as one of the standard events until 1962. It is part of the timed events in which the animals are given a "head start" from the mounted contestant. The fastest time wins. Tie-down roping, barrel racing, and steer wrestling are the other timed events.

Description

Team roping, the only rodeo event that features two contestants, requires close cooperation and teamwork between two highly skilled ropers—a header and a heeler. A header ropes the head, the heeler the heels. In this event, the contestants may be male or female, old or young. All can show off their skills. Some call it an "old man's game" because cowboys don't have to get off their horses. No matter who's in the saddle, horse and human reflexes must be fast.

The steer (allowed to be used in rodeos for one calendar year only) waits in a three-sided chute or "box" at one end of the arena. A nylon or elastic rope barrier is stretched across the end of the box and attached to the steer. On the steer's left is

Fig. 10.2.
It's a true team effort. The header positions the steer so that the heeler can slip the rope around its legs.
Photo by author.

the header, the cowboy on horseback who will rope the animal's head. On the steer's right waits the heeler, the roper who's in charge of lassoing legs.

When the header feels that the steer as well as his partner are ready for the chase, he nods to the gate keeper, who then releases the steer. Depending on the arena size, a certain amount of yardage, known as the advantage point—usually ten to fifteen feet—must be reached by the steer before the header starts out. When the steer reaches that point, the barrier is released, and the header takes off in pursuit. The heeler then follows the header out into the arena.

Once the steer bolts out of the chute, the header lassos the steer's head. Allowed only one of three legal catches, the header may catch the head and one horn, both horns, or around the neck. Any other catch is considered illegal and results in disqualification. After roping the steer, the header dallies (wraps his rope around the saddle horn two times), and turns the steer to the left, which causes its heels to fly in the air. This maneuver exposes the hind legs to the heeler. The header now pulls the steer behind him.

The heeler then attempts to rope both hind legs. He rounds the corner swinging his loop and throws his rope. If all goes according to plan, he catches two feet in the loop, then dallies up. Once the heeler has dallied and stopped his horse, the header must then turn his horse to face the heeler. With the ropes taut between the horses and the steer, the arena judge or flagman drops his flag to signal the timekeeper to stop the clock and record the team's time. A fast run in an average-sized rodeo arena is five to six seconds.

Scoring

As a timed event, the score and ultimately, winning depends on the fastest time. Record NFR in Las Vegas, Nevada, arena time is 3.7 seconds by the Williams/Skelton roping team in 1997.

Disqualification results when the header fails to rope his steer with the legal head catch. A no-score also results if the heeler fails to rope the steer's legs. If the heeler tosses his loop before the header has changed the direction of the steer, and has the animal still moving forward, a "crossfire," the team is disqualified.

Ten seconds are added when the header breaks the barrier before the steer has reached the advantage point. Some rodeos use heeler barriers, too. Five seconds are added if the heeler catches only one leg.

Each cowboy carries only one rope, but a total of three throws is allowed. Depending on the event, whether it's PRCA or amateur, a team may continue trying to rope the animal until they are successful, or they may decide to wait for another day when they accomplish their goal.

World record time is held by the team of Blaine Linaweaver and Jory Levy in San Angelo, Texas, in 2001—3.5 seconds.

The Header

"The header sets up everything," says Speed Williams. "If he does his job well, it makes it easy for the heeler to do his job." It's a true partnership and team effort. Williams stresses that the header's initial speed is paramount to a win. "How fast the person gets the animal" sets the tone for the entire run.

The Heeler

Precision and timing are the key ingredients to being a good heeler. Rich Skelton advises audiences to "watch how the heeler gets in time with the steer." When the animal's feet are off the ground, the heeler throws his loop. In this game, timing is everything.

Equipment and Clothing

As in any PRCA-sanctioned rodeo, cowboy hat, long-sleeved shirt fastened at the wrists and tucked in, western-cut jeans, and boots with spurs are required. The spurs used depend on the rider's horse, but usually blunted rowels do the trick.

Saddles have to be heavy enough to withstand a good jerk after the steer is roped. Most team-roping saddles, average cost of sixteen hundred dollars, are made from rawhide-covered wood. The saddle, specifically made for team roping, is designed to keep the roper in the saddle, which allows the roper to deliver the loop whenever he is ready. The saddle horn, officially called a dally post horn, is usually 3.5 inches high and wrapped with several strips of rawhide. This may be covered with rubber tubing to help protect the rawhide during roping. Rubber is much easier to replace than the saddle horn covering itself. Ropers go through several protective covers quickly.

A good saddle pad serves as a buffer between saddle and horse—working like a shock absorber. The pad needs to exceed the saddle by at least one inch so that when the front and flank cinches are tightened, the saddle never comes in direct contact with the horse's skin.

Breast collar and two cinches keep the saddle in place. "When the steer is roped and you dally, there is a great amount of pull inflicted on the saddle. This pressure will cause the saddle to slide forward onto the horse's neck," says Tee Woolman. When pulling the steer across the arena, even for a few feet, the weight of the steer pulls the saddle back. "The breast collar will become tight, keeping the saddle from rising up in the back when weight is applied to the front," adds Woolman. A front and back cinch keep the saddle in place.

In addition, splint boots guard against the horse striking and bruising the ankle. Bell boots, also called overreach boots, fit over the horse's front hooves to protect the front legs from being cut by the back hooves if the horse oversteps.

Leather horn wraps protect all team-roping cattle.

Fig. 10.3. *(top)*
The header catches the steer and maneuvers it into position.
PHOTO BY AUTHOR.

Fig. 10.4. *(bottom)*
It's up to the heeler to catch the steer's back legs.
PHOTO BY AUTHOR.

Header ropes and heeler ropes, naturally, are different sizes for their different uses. The header ropes tend to be softer than the heeler ropes. Usually now made of three- or four-strand nylon, the ropes use a honda, or rawhide loop located on the nylon, to keep the rope from burning through it. Cowboys have preference for ropes that work for them. However, according to rodeo contestant Judy Davis, "if he's a true roper, any rope will work."

The PRCA-required horn protector may be leather or nylon webbing. All roping steers wear the protective horn wrap. Nylon runs about seventeen dollars.

A roping glove may be made of cotton or deer skin and ranges in price from one dollar to thirty dollars. Material is personal preference, but the need for flexibility is important. During a busy weekend of roping, a cowboy may go through at least one pair of cotton gloves.

Injuries

Team ropers pride themselves on obtaining few injuries during their event. According to a Justin Sportsmedicine study covering ten years, of all rodeo injuries acquired, team ropers accounted for less than 1 percent. However, what usually gets hurt and the severity makes up for the lack of bruises and abrasions. The biggest injury is to the thumb when the cowboy dallies his rope—wraps it around the saddle horn. If he's not careful, or doesn't dally correctly, his thumb gets wrapped, too, and may be torn off. Other hand and wrist injuries and sprains make up the majority of the complaints.

The Steers

Corriente cattle, which originated in Mexico, are the preferred breed for team roping. These steers, averaging five hundred pounds, about seventy-five pounds heavier than other stock, have the right temperament—tough enough to accept repeated roping but gentle enough not to hurt the roper or his horse. They come out of the chute fast and hard, just what a cowboy needs for a good score.

The Horses

Just as important as the cowboys, the horses are part of the team effort. Without their cooperation, roping would be difficult if not impossible. The American quarter horse is the most popular among all rodeo competitors, especially team ropers. Horses are trained separately, header or heeler, and specialize in one of these tasks. Team-roping horses must have a high degree of "cow sense," being able to anticipate the steer's action and outmaneuver it. A good horse has intelligence in addition to physical alertness. They must possess the ability to stay calm right before entering the arena.

Heading horses are generally taller and heavier because they need power to turn the steer after it is roped.

Fig. 10.5.
A good "header" horse must have "cow sense" and lots of muscles.
PHOTO BY AUTHOR.

Smaller than their counterpart, heeling horses have to take corners during the event. Because of this, they need to be quick and agile, allowing them to better follow the steer and react to its moves.

Famous Team Ropers

It wasn't until 1995 that the PRCA recognized team-roping headers and heelers with separate world titles. Until that time, it was the team that was recognized.

Charles Maggini (1894–1982), won the first World Championship Team Roping and Steer Roping in 1929. He was inducted into the National Cowboy and Western Heritage Museum in Oklahoma City, Oklahoma, in 2003.

The Camarillo twins from Oakdale, California, were also inducted into the National Cowboy and Western Heritage Museum in Oklahoma City. Jerrold Camarillo won World Championship Team Roper titles from 1969 to 1977 and was inducted in 2003. Heeler Leo Camarillo won World Championship Team Roper titles in 1972, 1973, 1975, and 1983. He was inducted into the ProRodeo Hall of Fame

Fig. 10.6.
Team roping is a necessity of ranch work.
PHOTO BY AUTHOR.

in Colorado Springs, Colorado, in 1979, and National Cowboy and Western Heritage Museum in 1975.

Heeler Clay O'Brien Cooper of Texas qualified for the National Finals Rodeo in team roping twenty times and holds seven world titles. He was inducted into the ProRodeo Hall of Fame in 1997. In 2004, he came close to beating the world record by registering a 4.0 second run. His horse, nicknamed Ike, finished second as the PRCA/AQHA (American Quarter Horse Association) Team Roping Heel Horse of the Year in 2004.

Tee Woolman, a three-time world champion header from Texas, holds the world record for the fastest time—3.7 seconds. In addition to holding the world record, he was inducted into the ProRodeo Hall of Fame in Colorado Springs, Colorado, in 2004. He recommends practicing roping every day.

Rich Skelton encourages "doing what you enjoy for a living and making money at it." He says, "the more [practice] you put into it, the more you're going to get out of it." He should know: he and his former partner Speed Williams practiced every day. Skelton uses his favorite horse Chili Dog, voted the PRCA/AQHA Team Roping Heel Horse of the Year in 2004.

Skelton knows about practicing and winning. He's won eight world titles, setting a record with partner Williams for the most world titles and most consecutive world titles (1997–2004).

Speed Williams, originally from Florida but now residing in Texas, shares Skelton's world titles. Speed's first name is actually Ken, but it's the middle one, named after his father's friend, that fits like a glove. His record speaks for itself and his name—arena fastest time at 3.8. Besides being fast, he is one of only six ropers to head and heel at the National Finals Rodeo. He heeled for Casey Cox at the 1988 NFR.

How to Become a Team Roper

The key to success is hard work and endless practice. Team-roping partners must perfect their timing as a team, with their horses, and with the steers. Speed Williams and Rich Skelton stress practice, and both agree that a roping school, along with videos, is the best way to learn the art of roping.

You'll need a bale of hay with a practice head to start, a rope, a saw horse (to practice heeling), then a horse, boots for the horse, saddle, bridle, a pick-up, horse trailer, and of course feed for the horse. Skelton teaches the four basics of roping: position your horse, swing the rope, find your target, and deliver. He also advises "go to school, learn the basics, and get good work ethics—and keep practicing."

Roping schools are advertised through the Internet or at local feed and tack stores. Talk to other ropers to get advice on which school is best suited for you.

Associations

American Cowboys Team Roping Association
International Professional Rodeo Association
National High School Rodeo Association
National Intercollegiate Rodeo Association
North American Team Roping Association
Professional Rodeo Cowboys Association
United States Team Roping Championships
Women's Professional Rodeo Association

Team roping—a blur of precision like a well-oiled machine, a partnership between man and animals.

Fig. 11.1.
Tie-down roping is all about speed and willing animals.

11

Tie-Down Roping:
A Man and His Horse—
It's a Beautiful Thing

Tie-down roping showcases the best overall skills
of cowboys. It's the most complicated event in rodeo.
—Monty Lewis, 2004 WNFR World Champion Tie-Down Roper

WHAT SCREAMS "cowboy" more than galloping on horseback at full throttle across the open range to chase down a 250-pound calf? How about a calf charging out of the chute at breakneck speed followed closely on its heels by a cowboy swinging a lariat over his head? Tie-down roping, rodeo's most technical event, requires hours of practice to perfect the skills of both that cowboy and of his horse. Experts in the field contend that the unique blend of skills used by the cowboy and his horse make calf roping the most complex and difficult of rodeo's six most popular events. Competitive tie-down roping attracts some of rodeo's best athletes. Done right, it's like poetry in motion—in nine seconds.

History

Tie-down roping was a daily chore on ranches one hundred and sixty years ago in the Old West. The need for it hasn't changed at all today. Tie-down roping, formerly known as calf roping, is necessary for branding, doctoring, ear tagging, inspecting, or anything else a calf needs. A single cowboy on horseback heads out into the pasture or range, selects the calf, ropes it, and then does whatever needs doing. Calves are small and hornless, so a single man with a well-trained horse can perform the task at hand. The larger cattle require two people—team ropers. Ranch hands prided themselves on how fast they could rope the calves and naturally, turned their work into informal contests. Thus calf roping was born as a rodeo event.

Tie-down roping requires more than quickness and accuracy with a lasso, it also requires contestants to be experienced horsemen and fast sprinters. And people who like to practice—a lot.

Description

Calf roping is even more difficult than it appears, and involves several distinct skills executed in a very short amount of time. Good tie-down roping depends primarily on the teamwork between the cowboy and the horse. However, a feisty, uncooperative calf can outmaneuver even the best-oiled horse and cowboy team.

Two judges watch the action. The foul-line judge, or starter, waits near the box to catch the beginning action. The field judge farther down in the arena checks to be sure the calf is properly roped, flanked, and tied. Both may assess penalties either by fines, added time, or calling a *no-time*.

Fig. 11.2.
The calf must enter the arena before the mounted cowboy. Note the barrier cord on the ground.
PHOTO BY AUTHOR.

Fig. 11.3.
A good horse proves invaluable in assisting the roper.
Too much tension or not enough could cause disqualification.
PHOTO BY AUTHOR.

In this timed event, the mounted cowboy (or cowgirl) waits in a box, a three-sided fenced area adjacent to the chute holding the calf. The fourth side of the box opens into the arena. A breakaway nylon barrier is looped around the calf's neck and stretched across the open end of the rider's box. When the cowboy feels the time is right, he nods his head and the calf is released.

At this point, several things are put into motion. The calf bolts out of the chute, the cowboy starts swinging his lasso while still in the box, and the horse focuses on that little calf. When the calf reaches the advantage point, the head start given determined by the length of the arena, the barrier is released, and the cowboy and horse leap out of the box.

The cowboy makes his throw from horseback, jerks his slack to close the loop, and then "pitches his slack" to keep it out of the way of his mount. Once the calf is roped around the neck, the horse slides to a quick stop. After roping the calf, the cowboy makes a flying dismount, usually on the right side, while his horse backs up. The roper sprints and, using the rope anchored to his saddle horn as a guideline, follows the rope to his calf. If the animal is not standing, he must get it on its feet again and lift it high enough that the judges see daylight between the ground and its body, before continuing. The great calf ropers know precisely how to handle their rope so the calf is brought to a stop without falling.

The roper throws the calf on its side by hand (flanking) and grabs legs. Using a six-foot piggin' string (see Glossary) which has been clenched in his teeth, he then ties three legs together by putting the loop over a front leg, pushing the hind legs up and tying them with two wraps and a "hooey" (a halfhitch knot).

During this activity, the horse must pull back hard enough to eliminate any slack in the rope, otherwise the calf will jump up and take off. However, the horse cannot pull so hard that the calf is dragged off.

After tying the calf, the roper throws his hands in the air to signal the arena judge that the run is completed. The clock stops at this point. However, it's far from over. He must remount his horse, ride forward to create slack in the rope, then wait six seconds to see if the calf remains tied. If it stays bound, time is recorded, and hopefully money will be forthcoming. If the calf somehow manages to free itself, the roper receives a *no-time*.

Today's ropers save seconds by getting off the right side of the horse (normal procedure is off the left), thus not having to duck under the rope. This was first done in the 1960s by two right-handed ropers, and to their amazement, seconds were saved, thus qualifying them for the National Finals Rodeo. Since their technique worked, it has become standard in most roping events.

Additionally, time is shaved off the clock by switching the calf around so that its head faces the horse.

Scoring

The cowboy with the fastest time wins. It's just that simple. There is no judging for form of either the calf or the cowboy. However, the calf-leg tie must include one wrap and the "hooey." Nine seconds is considered a very good time.

There are only a few penalties that can be imposed during this event. A ten-second penalty is added if the calf roper breaks the barrier at the beginning of the run, before the calf reaches the advantage point. *No-time* is given if the calf breaks free after being roped during the six-second "waiting period." Of course, if the calf eludes the lasso completely, after thirty-five seconds time is called.

One penalty left up to the judges' discretion is that for a roped calf that is dragged or flips backward. Most horses will pull the calf a few inches, but if the horse drags the calf too far and/or endangers its well-being, such as by flipping it over, the judge may call time right then. A *no-time* is awarded, possibly a fine, and a stern lecture given the horse by the empty-pocketed cowboy.

World records are hard to break, and in the rodeo world that's true, too. Lee Phillips in Assiniboia, Saskatchewan, in 1978, roped his calf in 5.7 seconds. Cody Ohl roped in 6.5 seconds at the Wrangler National Finals Rodeo in 2003. Right behind him were Joe Beaver (West Jordan, Utah, 1986, then Dallas, Texas in 2001), and Stran Smith (Dallas, Texas, in 2001), both recording 6.7 seconds.

The Animals

"A horse is a really important part of tie-down roping," says 2004 WNFR Tie-Down Roping World Champion Monty Lewis. His horse Ned, thirteen, is still going strong. He reports that horses that are treated well and kept in good condition can continue to rope into their twenties.

The way the horse maneuvers is very important. He must rate the speed of the calf, stop on cue in a single stride, and then hold the rope taut while the roper runs to his calf. A solid, true working horse is difficult to find and commands a high price. Some well-trained calf-roping quarter horses fetch upwards of from 75,000 dollars to 100,000 dollars.

The horse must be fast enough to stay behind the calf at the proper interval and off to one side even if the calf turns and ducks. The horse must have "cow sense,"

Fig. 11.4.
Healthy stock ensures the competitor a good run at beating the clock.
PHOTO BY AUTHOR.

Fig. 11.5.
Calves must be weaned and will be used for one calendar year only.
PHOTO BY AUTHOR.

anticipating the calf's actions. Good roping horses fixate on the calf and stay focused throughout the event. Their ears cock forward and their eyes stay glued on their quarry. Many horses have short attention spans and must be reminded what their job is. Therefore, good roping horses are at a premium.

Calves must be native, Brahma, or a cross breed, and weigh between 220 and 280 pounds, about three times more than their birth weight. They must be weaned from their mothers and branded or ear-tagged. At this size and age, their hides are thicker than at birth and their bodies are flexible enough not to be injured during roping. Tie-down roping calves are used only about thirty times before they grow too large for this event.

According to statistics compiled by the Professional Rodeo Cowboys Association, out of 28 rodeos, or 33,991 animal exposures, just 16 were injured. That translates to an injury rate less than 0.00047, or less than one in 2,000. In this sport, the cowboy wishes those were *his* injury statistics!

Injuries

Injuries to tie-down ropers, calf ropers, account for 3 percent of all rodeo performers' injuries. "Legs, hands, knees, hips, and lower back," lists Monty Lewis. He stresses that the strain on the cowboys' hips when they sit down on the calves causes ropers to retire much sooner than they'd anticipated. More than one roper has undergone hip replacement surgery at a young age. In addition, Lewis explains, "The lower back gets sprained and pulled from flanking, and the shoulders dislocated and sore from swinging the ropes."

Twisted ankles, torn knees, and broken hands are the most common injuries to calf ropers. The ankles and knees can twist when the cowboy dismounts at full speed from his horse, and the knee may tear because he goes off on the right side. "There are always injuries that come with this sport," says Bill Blackwood, a New Mexico roper.

Thorough stretching before performance can help reduce the rate of injury.

Clothing and Equipment

As in all Professional Rodeo Cowboys Association–sponsored events, a dress code is enforced. Western-style long-sleeved shirts buttoned at the cuffs and tucked into jeans, cowboy hat, and boots are required. The spurs worn depend on the cowboy's preference with his horse. No chaps or protective vests are worn.

In fact, the only specialized apparel is the glove. The glove must be soft and pliable enough for the roper to expand the loop, then dally in milliseconds. Most gloves are cotton and sell for around one dollar. Deerskin gloves may run upwards of thirty dollars, but last longer than cotton, which may live out the weekend.

For the tie-down roper, the rope is the biggest consideration. Calf ropes are softer than those used for team roping, but whether they are three strands or four depends on the preference of the roper. Many ropers have different ropes for the various weather and arena conditions.

The piggin' string, the 6-foot rope used to tie the calf's legs, is three-eighths of an inch in diameter, and made of nylon or hemp. It costs about seven dollars.

Cotton ropes tend to "wilt" with wetter weather while the nylon ropes keep their shape longer. Ropers use talc, powder, to keep the ropes in good working order. Standard twenty-five-foot calf ropes run about twenty-two dollars.

In addition to powder, a "honda," a plastic or rawhide loop, is braided into the rope. This honda is where the end of the rope slips through and helps keep the rest of the rope from burning through the loop.

Calf-roping saddles are heavier than basic saddles due to the strain on the horse. The saddle horn, or dally post horn, is 3 ½ inches high and wrapped with extra rawhide. Rubber casings may be added over the additional rawhide strips to keep wear and tear down to a minimum. An average roping saddle costs

Fig. 11.6.
Besides his horse, the roper's most valuable asset is a good rope.
PHOTO BY AUTHOR.

sixteen hundred dollars. Stirrups may be wide or narrow, depending again on the cowboy's preference.

Roping horses need leg protection in the form of bell boots, or overreach boots, and splint boots. Bell boots and splint boots help protect the front legs from being bruised or cut by the back legs "overreaching" during a run. Splint boots average fourteen dollars, rubber bell boots ten dollars. Roper skid boots, which fasten around the "ankle" portion of the horse's legs, help keep him from twisting the ankle or pulling a muscle. These run about thirty-six dollars.

Famous Ropers

Calf roping is one event in which women were allowed to compete up through the early 1920s, then after reconfiguring associations and rules, and the founding of the Girls' Rodeo Association, women joined competitive rodeo once more.

Dixie Reger Mosely, born in 1905, was the youngest in a family of rodeo performers, and became the first juvenile professional clown while working Wild West Shows. Although she was a trick rider, her best rodeo event was calf roping. She was a charter member of the GRA and was inducted into the National Cowgirl Hall of Fame in Texas in 1982.

Jewel Frost Duncan, born in 1902, was the first woman roper to compete in the West of the Pecos Rodeo in 1929, and since she was the only woman, had to compete against the men. She was inducted into the National Cowgirl Hall of Fame in Texas in 1976.

Isora DeRacy Young, born in 1905, said she "would rather rope than eat." In the early part of the twentieth century, women participated under "contract." Despite that label, she went on to win against many men and win Queen of the Rodeo title. She was inducted into the National Cowgirl Hall of Fame in 1979.

Toots Mansfield won his first calf roping championship title in 1939 and followed it with championships in 1940, 1941, 1943, 1945, 1948, and 1950. He won the Madison Square Garden calf roping seven times. Mansfield was noted for his inordinate amount of consistency and speed. He rarely made mistakes and dismounted close to his horse, and grabbed the rope as a guideline. His favorite horse, the one that "had it all," was Honey Boy.

Joe Beaver has qualified for the Wrangler National Finals Rodeo in tie-down roping seventeen times beginning in 1985. He won the WNFR Tie-Down Roping World Championship in 1985, 1987, 1988, 1992, and 1993. In 2001, he won the Coors Original Fans Favorite Cowboy.

Making his mark on the tie-down roping world is Texan Monty Lewis. Newcomer Lewis won his first world title in 2004 after entering his first WNFR in seventh place. He won the aggregate title with a total time of 87.8 seconds on 10 head (less than 4 seconds off the WNFR record).

After winning the 2004 WNFR World Tie-Down Championship in Las Vegas, Monty Lewis drove back home to Texas not only with a new buckle and title, but with ninety-three thousand dollars in his pocket. In addition to Lewis's World Title, his horse, Ned, thirteen, took home the prized title of PRCA/AQHA Tie-Down Roping Horse of the Year.

"I'm happy it turned out that way," Lewis admitted. But good roping and winning take a lot of hard work and mental concentration. "You just gotta be there. But you have to be a cowboy to do it." Calf roping requires the cowboy to be skilled not

Fig. 11.7.
This New Mexico State University Rodeo Team member
practices so they can qualify at the national level.
PHOTO BY AUTHOR.

only with a rope but with a horse, Lewis explains. "And, you have to be athletic to run on the ground."

When asked about the future, Lewis chuckled. "Hopefully I keep winning. My goal is to win the Gold when I'm old . . . 40."

How to Become a Tie-Down Roper

While calf roping looks easy, it's so technical that hundreds of hours of practice and commitment are required to be competitive. But just learning is fun. There are many roping schools around the United States, Canada, and Australia. However, a bale of hay, a practice calf head (yes, there's such a thing), a couple of ropes, and someone to show you how to throw is all that's necessary to begin.

Check the Internet or local feed and tack stores for ropers giving lessons or schools. Generally, an hour-long lesson averages thirty-five dollars.

Associations

Professional Rodeo Cowboys Association
United States Calf Ropers Association
Women's Professional Rodeo Association

Tie-down roping—true magic at lightning speed. A partnership between man and horse. But who can describe it better than Monty Lewis? "Calf roping's the *best* event—ever!"

Fig. 12.1.
Riders reach speeds of thirty miles per hour on a good horse.
Photo by author.

Barrel Racing: Winning by a Woman's Nose

The best part of barrel racing is being a team
with your horse, and making it work.
—Charmayne James, eleven times World Champion Barrel Racer

HAIRPIN TURNS AROUND BARRELS AT THIRTY MILES PER HOUR. Spirited horse. A timer ticking away milliseconds. Hooves pounding. Boot heels thumping against the horse's skin. More speed. Leaning with the horse. Faster. Barrel Racing. Rodeo style.

History
Barrel racing is one of rodeo's newest events and was initially considered a sideline activity of traditional rodeo. Today, however, it is considered an integral part of most rodeos. Equine athletes and skilled horsewomen thrill audiences, and according to polls, rank just behind bull riding in crowd popularity.

The general consensus about the invention of barrel racing is that cowboy wives and girlfriends needed "something to do" while their men competed in rodeo events, so the women got together for some friendly competition. Another version of the origin is that cowgirls got together to see who could whip around obstacles fastest, an amiable challenge of horsemanship. Either way, barrel racing is another exhilarating sport that grew out of the competitive spirit of the West.

In 1948, a group of Texas women, led by Blanch Altizer-Smith, sister of 1959 PRCA (Professional Rodeo Cowboys Association) calf-roping champion Jim Bob Altizer, joined forces to bring the sport of barrel racing into the rodeo arena. Known as the Girls' Rodeo Association (GRA), there were seventy-four charter members with sixty approved events. The first year's payoff totaled twenty-nine thousand dollars.

The GRA was renamed in 1982, and since then, the Women's Professional Rodeo Association (WPRA) has expanded its goals to include larger purses, bigger and better rodeos, and greater public recognition.

Description

Barrel racing is one woman, one horse, three barrels, and a timer. The horse is ridden as quickly as possible around three barrels in a cloverleaf pattern. After circling the third barrel, horse and rider gallop toward the finish line. The judge is that stopwatch. However, an arena or events judge calls the official time tally and adds penalty seconds, if necessary.

For an event, the arena's ground is raked and smoothed, then three barrels are set up at the marked locations. A barrel is set on the right and another one on the left side of the arena from where the rider enters, a third near the back of the arena, thus creating a triangle. The front barrels, set across from each other, must have a minimum of fifteen feet between each of them and the side fence (according to National Barrel Horse Association—NBHA—rules). The third barrel must have a minimum

Fig. 12.2.
Barrels are placed in a triangular pattern. Racers ride in a cloverleaf pattern as fast as possible. Fifteen seconds is considered a good time.
Photo by author.

of thirty feet between it and the back fence. The first barrel must be at least thirty feet from the timer line.

The rider then enters the arena at full speed, rounds each barrel, and then exits where she entered. A stopwatch or electronic timer is used and registers down to a hundredth of a second. According to barrel-racing world champion Charmayne James, a horse running from the third barrel to the timer line averages twenty-eight to thirty-four miles per hour.

When the rider enters the arena, she can choose to start with either of the front two barrels. Horses, like people, have dominant right or left sides, "right- or left-hoofed, so to speak." Therefore, a rider is allowed to take either barrel first, depending on whether her horse is stronger turning right or left. A pattern starting with the right turn around the right-hand barrel must be followed by two left turns. A rider who chooses to go left must make two right-hand turns for the second and third barrel. Either start produces the desired cloverleaf pattern.

Depending on the size of the arena, the times will vary, but a good run in a standard-size arena that measures 130 feet by 200 feet would be under 17.50 seconds. Generally a winning time is 13 to 14 seconds. The barrels themselves are standard metal or heavy plastic that withstand hauling around and being knocked over. The first barrel a rider navigates is commonly called the "money barrel" because this turn often decides the outcome of the race.

Riders

Barrel-racing participants compete in one of two divisions—girls twelve and under compete in the novice division, thirteen and older in the women's division. The PRCA does not include barrel racing in its organization, but women may belong. The WPRA includes barrel racing and is often invited to PRCA-sanctioned rodeos, thus creating a well-rounded rodeo.

Although barrel racing is considered a women's sport, men can participate alongside the women. Some are successful, but women have the advantage of being lighter in a sport where speed is paramount. Since barrel racing is not part of the PRCA and men are not allowed to join the WPRA, finding professional male barrel racers may be difficult.

Age is not a factor in barrel racing. Some girls start racing as soon as they can sit upright in a saddle, while some don't begin until adulthood. Young or old, male or female, those who want to race must be willing to ride twenty-five to thirty miles per hour at a full out run and to risk falling off a speeding horse.

Equipment and Clothing

Dress codes are enforced at rodeos or western riding events at the national level, especially those sanctioned by the WPRA, NBHA, or PRCA. Riders must wear a western hat,

Fig. 12.3.
Barrel racers become one with the horse to beat the clock.
Photo by Myke Groves.

long-sleeve shirt, and cowboy boots. Sleeves must be rolled down and buttoned or snapped, and shirttails must be tucked in. Local and regional events may have additional requirements such as chaps or shotguns (long, narrow chaps). Riders twelve years old and under must wear safety helmets at sanctioned events. Riders may elect to wear spurs, neckties, or other items. Thick, plastic shin guards are highly recommended so that when the rider's leg contacts the barrel, bruising is minimized.

Besides a horse, a rider needs only a saddle and bridle. A novice rider needs a helmet. As an amateur, a rider may use any type of saddle, western or English, but once she breaks into the open ranks in the WPRA, she must use a western saddle.

Specially made barrel racing saddles, averaging one thousand to twelve hundred dollars, are approximately twenty pounds lighter than the standard roping saddle and feature a rounded skirt to give the horse's flanks more room to maneuver. The pommel (the area where the saddle horn rests) is wider to accommodate the rider's thighs. A barrel racer may slide forward, which helps to stop the momentum. The horn itself is about five inches high and thin enough for a woman's hand to easily grip. The cantle, or back part of the seat, is a bit deeper and narrower than a traditional roping saddle.

Saddle blankets or pads are important for a good run. The pad needs to be breathable to allow the horse to sweat evenly. Special racing pads are available. Some riders use a breastplate or collar across the horse's chest. This breastplate keeps the saddle from sliding off backward during a race. These can be basic leather or ornately carved and embedded with silver.

Some racers also use "tie-downs," a leather strap attaching the bridle to the breastplate that keeps the horse's head from rearing up. If a horse's head is too high, he's looking up and not focusing on the next barrel. Chances are he's thinking about that exit.

Hoof covers or "overreach boots" wrap around the horse's front hooves and serve as protection. Velcro or metal fasteners attach the boots in the front of the

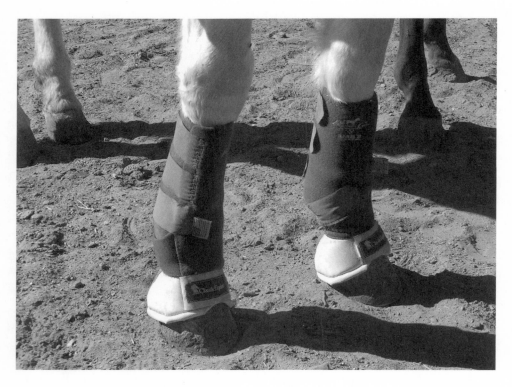

Fig. 12.4.
Every precaution is taken to ensure animals' safety.
These splint and overreach boots protect the horse's legs.
PHOTO BY AUTHOR.

hoof and cover it completely. These are used on horses whose back legs tend to kick or nick their front ones when running. This tendency can result in bruising, cuts, and in worse cases, sliced tendons. Also called bell boots, these leather protectors may cost upwards of ninety-five dollars, but are well worth the price. Shin wraps, or splint boots, wrap around the horse's lower legs, adding support to the tendons and helping to prevent shin splints.

About half the riders use quirts or whips. Many horses are trained for voice command, which makes quirts unnecessary. The riders who use them, however, do not hurt the animal. The thump on the horse's flanks serve only as a signal for the horse to run.

Some racers feel their horse has the incentive and training to run by voice command and therefore they do not use spurs. However, racers who do use spurs wear those with blunt rowels and short shanks. The rowels are allowed to roll and are not tied with wire such as those the bull riders use. The blunt rowels do not injure the animal and, like quirts, they cue the horse to run. There are no sharp objects, but a nudge with this "moves the horse's attention" to the fact he needs to run. The relationship between horse and rider is tantamount to successful racing; therefore, whether the rider uses spurs and quirts or not depends on the horse and the rider understanding each other. (For more on spurs, see Glossary.)

Horses

The breed for a good barrel racer is not as essential as in other areas such as cutting and horseracing. Several great barrel racers have been of unknown heritage. But they must be swift and intelligent enough to avoid tipping over the barrels. Also, the horse must be able to withstand long hours in the trailer traveling from rodeo to rodeo. Cowgirls spend endless hours in the truck and the horse must be a good traveler, too. If a horse is fast, competitive, and reacts well to the demands of travel, he could be a real winner.

Choosing a winning horse can be difficult, but a quarter horse is a good place to start. Quarter horses are so named because they were originally bred to sprint a quarter mile at a time. These horses have good acceleration and the proper attitude for barrel racing. They're quick learners and are usually even tempered, not high spirited like the thoroughbreds. In addition, their heavier rumps provide better balanced rides and their short, compact pasterns (part of the foot between the fetlock and hoof— ankle) reduce the threat of injury to their legs. Morgans, Appaloosas, paint horses, and even Arabians are also good for this sport. A proven barrel-racing horse can cost fifty thousand dollars, and that's before the veterinarian and feed bills.

Horseshoes specially made for barrel racing are available but not required. They are lighter than average shoes and equipped with cleats that help the horse grip the arena dirt. Used only for barrel racing, these shoes are time consuming to put on and take off, so many riders opt not to use them.

Fig. 12.5.
Horses are painstakingly trained to turn in
close to the barrel, but not knock it over.
PHOTO BY AUTHOR.

Horses destined for barrel racing should be at least five years old. Before that, their bones and muscles haven't matured enough. Gentle riding and training is advisable to start them on their way to fame. Training for barrel racing includes trail or country rides. Once the rider and horse are comfortable with each other, then it's time to head into the arena for some barrel practice.

Scoring

Barrel-racing scoring is simplistic. A rider enters the arena, rides past the timer at the time line, circles three barrels, then exits over the same line. Electronic timers report the seconds from line to line. The closer to a barrel the racer rides and the straighter the line between the barrels, the faster the time. The rider is allowed to grip the saddle horn and/or touch the horse during the race.

Only two incidents can add to the rider's time: knocking over a barrel or not running the prescribed course. A barrel may be touched and may wobble with no penalty, but if it falls, five seconds are added to the final time. A rider is automatically disqualified if the horse does not go around all three barrels in the cloverleaf pattern.

Barrel-racing horses and riders are not judged on their appearance. No particular grooming rules or requirements exist. However, a rider may braid her horse's mane and tail to prevent interference during the race.

In some racing events, if a rider's hat comes off during the run, she is assessed a fine, usually fifteen dollars.

How to Become a Barrel Racer

Anyone can race barrels. All that is needed is a horse, barrels, and a place to ride. Success is a matter of practice, practice, practice. Great success depends on becoming one with the horse—becoming a team.

Many barrel-racing schools are available across the country. Most can be found listed on the Internet. Check with the local rodeo association, barrel-racing association, or feed and tack stores for recommendations.

Barrel-racing clinics are held around the country by world champion racers. Charmayne James runs a clinic several times a year but limits the enrollment to thirty riders at a time. She does that so she can give individual attention to each rider.

Fig. 12.6.
Electronic timers are set at the arena entry,
sending the "official" time to the arena judges.

Bill Dunigan in Maryland also offers barrel-racing clinics. Martha Josey, the only woman to qualify for the National Finals Rodeo in four consecutive decades, hosts the nationally recognized World Champion Junior Barrel Race. Barrel racers today may look forward to winning big bucks. During the 2004 racing season, the leader in the Jack Daniel's World Standings for Barrel Racing won over ninety-two thousand dollars. In fact, in 1999 at the National Finals Rodeo in Las Vegas, Nevada, Sherry Cervi (two time World Champion Barrel Racer) won twenty-five thousand dollars more than the next highest money winner, a man. In that year, she took home the highest season earnings check of any professional rodeo athlete, man or woman.

Associations

Alberta Barrel Racing Association (ABRA)—largest barrel racing association in Canada
American Barrel Racing Association
American West 4D
National Barrel Horse Association (NBHA)
National High School Rodeo Association (NHSRA)
National Intercollegiate Rodeo Association (NIRA)
Women's Professional Rodeo Association (WPRA)

Tony Garritano, manager of Charmayne James, best summarized the sport: "It's all about speed." Barrel racing. Three barrels, one woman, one horse, one stopwatch.

Fig. 13.1.
Flags wave and adrenaline pumps at the WRCA grand entry in Amarillo,
Texas. Twenty ranches from the United States and Canada entered.
PHOTO BY MYKE GROVES.

13

Rodeos—They're Everywhere

Every rodeo requires an entry fee (for the cowboy) and promises nothing.
—Anonymous

RODEOS HAPPEN EVERYWHERE AND AT JUST ABOUT ANY TIME OF YEAR—inside, outside, organized, or impromptu. No way is it possible to provide a comprehensive listing of the thousands of rodeos held around the country, but a few are listed at the end of this chapter. The following are some of the better-known rodeos. Check your local feed and tack store, rodeo association, or visit the Internet for further information.

The Big Ones

Rodeos all have the same ingredients—animals, cowboys, cowgirls, thrills, spills, and heart-stopping action. However, even though the scenery and locations change, the adrenaline is there. If possible, attend a local rodeo, and then take in one of these larger ones. You won't be sorry.

The First Annual Stock Show took place along Marine Creek in North Fort Worth, Texas, in 1896. Held in conjunction with the National Livestock Exchange Convention in October, a parade was organized to accompany the festivities. Thus the **Fort Worth Stockshow and Rodeo** was born, called back then the Texas Fat Stock Show.

Its history is as wide and varied as the contestants and livestock featured today. Back in 1904, Bill "Dusky Demon" Pickett invented bulldogging, demonstrating his amazing steer lip-biting technique. He bit the bull's lip and wrestled it to a standstill. Then in 1905, the round-up or regular ranch work was billed as a "Wild West Performance," where premiums and prizes were sought for the first time. Admission in 1907 was a whopping twenty-five cents. The Northside Coliseum was billed as "the most opulent and dynamic livestock pavilion in the entire Western Hemisphere." It featured skylights, incandescents, and patriotic flags, and the event's name was changed to National Feeders and Breeders Show.

In 1909, the parade featured forty Comanche and Kiowa men led by Chief Quanah Parker. It was also the first and last time prize show bulls were featured in the parade. One can only imagine what happened that day.

The Fat Livestock Show continued to grow in leaps and bound through world wars, the depression, changes of political leaders, and improved breeding programs.

Fig. 13.2.
Bulls are safest when behind iron fences. Imagine
a herd of these running down the streets of Fort Worth.
Photo by Myke Groves.

It wasn't until 1987, however, that its name officially became Southwestern Exposition and Livestock Show. In 2002, a record 951,000 visitors attended the show with over 24,000 head of livestock entered (fourteen livestock sales generated over four million dollars).

The Fort Worth Livestock Show and Rodeo runs from mid-January through mid-February and offers something for everybody. Llama as well as Angus bull sales, beef heifer shows, poultry shows, junior livestock shows, sheep, pigs, and of course horse shows round out the events. The Texas Cowboy Poet Association offers their poetry while music competitions and exhibitions are ever present. The "world's original indoor rodeo" offers the traditional rodeo events.

Ticket prices are family-oriented and as Fort Worth is a large city, lodging is bountiful.

Who knew back in 1906 that llamas, yaks, and bison would be included in the Denver, Colorado, livestock show? One can bet the livestock commissioners didn't see this one coming. The first show opened in that year and ran for six days. Attendance was estimated at fifteen thousand. Also in that year, the grand champion steer sold for thirty-three cents a pound, twenty-three cents over market price. The name changed to the **Western Stock Show Association**, which retains that moniker today.

In 1911, they added the first beef carcass contest as well as its first poultry show. In 1919, the Brown Palace Hotel paid a record fifty cents a pound for the grand champion steer. Ticket prices were raised in 1920 from twenty-five cents to seventy-five cents and attendance reached over 100,000.

The first rodeo held in conjunction with the livestock show occurred in 1932. Total rodeo prize money distributed was seventy-three hundred dollars. In 1945, two Hereford bulls were sold for fifty thousand dollars *each*, a record for breeding cattle at that time.

While attendance has soared over time, one year it took a nosedive. In 1978, the Denver Broncos football team had made it to the Super Bowl for the first time, and "Broncomania" swept the state. Attendance plunged by 12,500. However, by 1981 crowds surged to 360,000, where also a record of 301,000 dollars, paid for a Hereford bull, still stands today.

The show was expanded to include fourteen days in 1988, which brought in over 500,000 people. The Mexican Rodeo Extravaganza, premiering in 1995 in the Denver Coliseum, was a sell out. The Working Stock Dog competition began the same year. By 1997, a record twenty-three breeds of cattle were on sale or shown. In December of that year, the National Western was selected as the world's number one Indoor Rodeo of ProRodeo Cowboy's Association convention.

So what about yaks? Elk and yak sales were added to the livestock sales program in 1999. The Olympic qualifying competition for the U.S. Equestrian Reining Horse

Fig. 13.3.
Rodeo is a family affair. Cody Sifford of Corrales, New Mexico, enjoys a rodeo hot dog and anticipates riding a sheep, known as "mutton busting." PHOTO BY HALEY CRAWFORD.

Team made its debut the same year. Not to be outdone by yaks and horses, the Colorado Rocky Mountain Fiddle Championships were held there for the first time in 2003. The show's attendance by then had soared to over 641,000. They're probably still counting noses.

The National Western Livestock Show offers many different types of animals for public inspection and entertainment. The show's officials state that "we continue striving to meet the obligation of our original charter, which is education, as well as meeting the challenge of innovation in the arena of family entertainment." What can be more entertaining than a bison or yak show?

Yaks, originally from the Himalayas and the center point of Tibetan culture, were introduced to North America over a hundred years ago. They are known as lean-meat producers, especially when bred with cattle.

Llamas will be displayed and compete at one of the oldest and largest shows in North America. Youth and adult performance classes are judged by the ability of the llama to navigate through obstacle courses. Halter classes judge llamas for conformation, disposition, and overall soundness. Llamas, originally from South America, are members of the camel family and are raised for packing, wool production, cart pulling, exhibitions, guardians of livestock herds, and 4-H projects.

Sanctioned by the National Bison Association, the Gold Trophy Bison Show and Sale is the only bison show of this type in the world. The first bison, wrongly called buffalo, were shown and judged at this National Western show in 1980 and have continued as a welcomed addition. Bison are not led into the ring like cattle, but bison are judged in the yards and this event draws a huge crowd. The center of life for the Plains Indians, bison were almost hunted to extinction (an estimated sixty million had been reduced to one thousand in 1893), but have rebounded today. Bison provide food, clothing, shelter, and are a part of Native American spiritual celebrations.

In addition to the more exotic animals, the National Western Stock Show offers a market place for more than nineteen different breeds of cattle. And, while not judging livestock, people can watch the PRCA rodeo, which includes bronc riding, bull riding, tie-down roping, team roping, steer wrestling, and barrel racing. The Professional Bull Riders (PBR) compete for prize money during a few of the rodeo events.

Denver, Colorado, is a huge city with thousands of motel/hotel rooms. Ticket prices are reasonable and with lodging available, the National Western Stock Show provides an exciting alternative to cold January days. Check the Internet for ticket prices and further information.

"The Rodeo Capital of the World," Cody, Wyoming, boasts the only nightly rodeo in the country, **The Cody Nite Rodeo.** Held annually from June 1 through August 31, this rodeo features bareback riding, saddle bronc riding, barrel racing, steer wrestling, team roping, and tie-down roping, and then caps off with bull riding. In addition to these standard events, this rodeo offers Novice Barrel Race for kids under twelve, steer riding for those under fourteen, and a calf scramble where audience children may participate by trying to snatch a ribbon off a calf.

Cody Nite Rodeo was started in 1938 by Carly Downing, a member of Buffalo Bill's Wild West Show. Professional cowboys need to get a start somewhere, and for many of them, this rodeo is it. Cody Nite Rodeo, unofficially considered the "minor league" of the pro rodeo circuit, draws in cowboys and cowgirls on the verge of fame and fortune. This year, contestants who are athletic daredevils in their own right will vie for total prize money of 180,000 dollars.

During the summer, the Cody Nite Rodeo goes dark only during the Buffalo Bill Cody Stampede Rodeo, July 1–4. This "Cowboy Christmas," as contestants often call it, draws top cowboys and cowgirls from all over the country to see who walks away with the largest cash purse.

Over Labor Day weekend, Cody's Stampede Park hosts the "Iron Man" Rodeo in which ten cowboys compete in every single event. The only change from the nightly

Fig. 13.4.
Calf roping, a mainstay of rodeo, comes directly from ranch chores.
PHOTO BY MYKE GROVES.

rodeo is that team roping is replaced by a one-man version called "steer stopping," an event not to be forgotten.

The Cody Nite Rodeo, staged at 8:30 P.M., is located at Stampede Park in west Cody (US Highway 14/16). Tickets range from eight to fifteen dollars and are available at the gate after 7:00 P.M. or at many Cody businesses during the day. Prime seating is in the "Buzzard's Roost," perched above the bucking chutes. Parking is free. Concessions and a rodeo store in the park offer souvenirs as well as cowboy hats for sale. After the rodeo, spectators are invited to get cowboy and bullfighter (clown) autographs.

Due to the town's size, hotel/motel rooms are at a premium in Cody during the summer. Reservations well in advance are recommended. Touted as the longest running rodeo, visitors to Wyoming can easily fit this heart-stopping spectacle into their agenda. Cody Nite Rodeo is a must-see for everyone.

The **Calgary Stampede**, held in Calgary, Alberta, Canada, started life with Guy Weadick, a promoter and one-time roper for the 101 Ranch Wild West Show. He offered a purse of twenty thousand dollars in gold to cowboys who would cross the border and compete.

It all started in 1883 with the arrival of the railroad. Work slows in summer, so they decided that would be a great time for farmers and ranchers to hold an event to bring in tourists and with them, dollars. So, early July it was. In 1912, Weadick arranged financing and produced the first Calgary Stampede.

In 1922, the Calgary Industrial Exhibition was held and the next year joined forces with the rodeo. Thus—Calgary Exhibition and Stampede was christened the official name. It was in 1923 that the Stampede hosted the first competitive Chuckwagon Races. Audiences grew, competitors increased, and the purses expanded. In 1976, the Stampede attendance surpassed one million people. In 2000, attendance topped at 1,218,851! Must be that clear Canadian air.

Besides the air, the Calgary Stampede offers nine heats of four wagons and sixteen outriders who compete in what is billed as the GMC Rangeland Derby. Most people call it the Chuckwagon Races, one of the original events. Following the races are the grandstand shows, which are followed by fireworks. The PRCA-sanctioned rodeo offers bronc riding, bull riding, barrel racing, tie-down roping, and steer wrestling. In addition, the Calgary Stampede is the first one-million-dollar regular season professional rodeo.

Stampede tickets include the rodeo and chuckwagon races, but admittance is for the date on the ticket. Officials recommend allowing at least two days to take in all the excitement. A train runs from the town of Calgary to the rodeo site, where parking is limited and costly.

Check local listings for lodging accommodations, transportation, and exchange rates.

Who can resist free pancakes, grand parades, and rodeo? Lots and lots of rodeo. **Cheyenne Frontier Days,** "The Daddy of 'em All," is indeed a patriarch of rodeos with a history full of stories. And what stories he tells!

It all started when cowboys came off the range in the 1870s looking for a place to let off a little steam. What better place than Cheyenne, Wyoming, the quintessential Wild West town? In 1897, a Union Pacific Railroad agent decided a good way to promote his passenger tourist business would be entertainment in this dusty cow town. He planned "pitching and bucking contests," horse racing, and roping events. Thus it was in 1897 that the first Cheyenne Frontier Days was held and soon became *the* place for rodeo.

It didn't resemble Cheyenne's rodeo today. Visitors would park their buggies and wagons around the perimeter of a large pasture, unpack their picnic

Fig. 13.5.
Flags from various states as well as Canada bring spectators
and contestants together under one roof.
Photo by Myke Groves.

lunch, and watch the action. There were no standard events nor a standard method of judging. It would be a number of years before fancy chutes and grandstands were added.

From there it's grown into a supersize rodeo in the state with the least amount of population. Cheyenne, a city boasting fifty-three thousand residents, more than doubles in size during this seven-day event. Visitors from all fifty states and several foreign countries converge on Cheyenne in July.

Did someone say free pancakes? Three days during the week, free pancakes and ham, plus coffee, is offered to anyone who wants it. Held along a couple of downtown blocks, it's close enough to rodeo action, but far enough away for those pancakes not to be enshrouded in dust. A single-day record was set in 1996 when the Kiwanis volunteers served 16,897 people within a couple of hours. During that week, 40,000 people were fed in a total serving time of eight hours, ten minutes. If that's not impressive enough, the volunteers this year will flip more than 100,000 pancakes made from 5,000 pounds of mix, cook 3,000 pounds of ham, serve 9,200 cartons of milk, brew 520 gallons of coffee, and top it off with 630 pounds of butter and 475 gallons of syrup. And you thought your kids ate a lot!

Cheyenne Frontier Days is the largest rodeo in the country, not only in terms of free pancakes but also as far as contestants. Close to two thousand cowboys and cowgirls compete for bragging rights and a little bit of pocket change. Fancy belt buckles or hand-tooled saddles top off the awards. And the rodeo prides itself on nonstop action—chuckwagon cook-offs, parades, Indian Village, Wild Horse Gulch (old Western town), top-notch country entertainers, and of course, world-class PRCA rodeo events.

In 1896, just after the second Frontier Days rodeo, it was decided that American Indians were an important part of the American West and would make a welcomed addition to this spectacle. Their dances, traditions, and crafts have found a home in Cheyenne. The Cheyenne Frontier Days—truly something for everyone.

Tickets are reasonably priced, but hotel/motel rooms are at a premium. Because of Cheyenne's size, many people stay in Denver and then commute to Cheyenne, a mere 110 miles away. Make plans and reservations well in advance of July.

Following a 1909 Fourth of July celebration in Pendleton, Oregon, community leaders decided an annual rodeo event made good business sense. They called it the **Pendleton Round-Up** and offered bronc riding, horse racing—even fireworks. It was decided to hold this extravaganza in September, so that grain farmers could complete their harvest, and the livestock people could make their late summer stock check. In 1910, the Northwestern Frontier Exhibition Association elected its first president and established admission prices from $1.50 for a box, down to fifty cents for anyone on horseback or children under twelve.

Local Indians played a large role in the Round-Up, but only a handful competed. In 1916, Jackson Sundown, nephew to Chief Joseph, competed in the saddle bronc semi-final round. In the final round, the horse bucked and spun, but did not unseat Jackson Sundown. Thus, Sundown became the Pendleton Round-Up Champion Bronc Rider—at the age of fifty-two.

The Happy Canyon night show, premiering in 1915, embraces the founding of Oregon through the eyes of the Native Americans and emigrants, and offers a look back at history.

In 1918, the Round-Up showed a net profit of 5,098 dollars, which, by unanimous vote, was donated to the American Red Cross.

In today's world, what better way to spend a few September days than watching PRCA rodeo, watching Wild West reenactors "shoot it out" along Main Street, eating breakfast and barbecue, or watching the Tribal Ceremonial Dancing Contest, then the American Indian Beauty Contest?

Pendleton is a moderately sized town with limited accommodations. Advance reservations are recommended. Ticket prices are family friendly.

Fig. 13.6.
The Working Ranch Cowboy Association strives
to maintain and promote western values and lifestyles.
PHOTO BY MYKE GROVES.

Fig. 13.7.
Rodeo is hard work. This saddle bronc cowboy checks
his gear and mentally prepares before his ride.
PHOTO BY HALEY CRAWFORD.

Watch real ranch hands show off at the **Working Ranch Cowboy Championship Finals** in Amarillo, Texas, every November. With its humble beginning in 1995, the Working Ranch Cowboys Association has offered ranch teams from Canada and the United States a chance to compete for saddles, buckles, money, and braggin' rights. Other ranch rodeos are held throughout the year, but similar to the Wrangler National Finals Rodeo, the best of the best meet in Amarillo for good-natured sparring.

For four days, twenty teams of working ranch cowboys compete in team penning, doctoring, and branding as well as wild cow milking (a not-to-be-missed spectacle). Bronc riding as accomplished on a ranch is also part of the rodeo. This event is the only portion of the rodeo that is not performed by the entire team.

Tickets are reasonably priced and include admission to the Trade and Trappings Expo, Pokey the Clown show, and the rodeo itself. Amarillo is large enough to provide lodgings for anyone who attends the WRCA Championship, but motels close by fill up quickly. Check the Internet for further information or contact the Working Ranch Cowboys Association for tickets.

Although Deer Trail, Colorado, claims fame as the original source of rodeo, the **Wrangler National Finals Rodeo** held in Las Vegas, Nevada, has claims of its own. Close to eight thousand cowboys in the PRCA (Professional Rodeo Cowboys Association) compete year long for inclusion in this ten-day event. It's what the Super Bowl is to football. Only the best make it this far.

In 1959, the first National Finals Rodeo was held in Dallas, followed by Los Angeles (1962–64), and Oklahoma City (1965–84). The championship found a home in Las Vegas in 1985 and the rest, as they say, is history.

Seven events comprise the National Finals: bareback bronc riding, saddle bronc riding, tie-down roping, steer wrestling, barrel racing, team roping, and the ever-popular bull riding.

Rodeo cowboys' lives are filled with travel, working out, and long-distance relationships. The end result, however, is money . . . a lot of it. In 2003, All-Around Cowboy Trevor Brazille took home just shy of 300,000 dollars. The 2004 World Champion Bareback rider, Kelly Timberman, netted over 225,000 dollars. Not bad for winning eight seconds at a time.

The PRCA recognizes that the media, especially coverage by a couple national networks, has propelled rodeo's recognition and appreciation by the general populace. Sweden, Russia, and Australia watch the WNFR, also.

Las Vegas, Nevada, is rich in hotel/motel rooms. Lodging is easy to find, but tickets to the WNFR can be a bit pricey and hard to wrangle. But whatever the price, it's well worth it.

Rodeo—the quintessential Western sparring match. For over one hundred years it has entertained, enthralled, excited, and inspired people from all walks of life. Let's hope it stays around for several hundred more.

Location, Location, Location—Rodeos by Month

January

    Black Hills Stock Show and Rodeo—Rapid City, South Dakota
    California Circuit Finals—Norco, California
    Fort Worth Stockshow and Rodeo—Fort Worth, Texas
    Homestead Championship Rodeo—Homestead, Florida
    Mudgee—New South Wales, Australia
    National Western Stockshow and Rodeo—Denver, Colorado
    Tuff Hedeman Louisiana Shootout—Bossier City, Louisiana
    Turquoise Circuit Finals—Lake Havasu City, Arizona

February

    Dixie National Rodeo—Jackson, Mississippi

    Federation West Championship Rodeo—Sedalia, Missouri

    Fiesta de los Vaqueros—Tucson, Arizona

    Fort Worth Stockshow and Rodeo—Fort Worth, Texas

    PRCA Championship Rodeo—Council Bluffs, Iowa

    San Antonio Stock Show and Rodeo—San Antonio, Texas

    Silver Spurs Semi-Annual Rodeo—Kissimmee, Florida

    Southwestern International Livestock Show & Rodeo—El Paso, Texas

March

    Dodge National Circuit Finals—Pocatello, Idaho

    Houston Livestock Show and Rodeo—Houston, Texas

    Kyabram—Victoria, Australia

April

    Laughlin River Stampede—Laughlin, Nevada

Fig. 13.8.
Not everything about rodeo is glamorous. Maintaining good
arena grounds is paramount to a successful rodeo.
PHOTO BY AUTHOR.

May

Lincoln County Ranch Rodeo—Memorial Day in Capitan, New Mexico

Old Fort Days Rodeo—Fort Smith, Arkansas

June

Buffalo PRCA Rodeo—Buffalo, Minnesota

Cody Nite Rodeo—Cody, Wyoming—longest running rodeo

Colorado Championship Ranch Rodeo—Hugo, Colorado

Flint Hills Rodeo—Strong City, Kansas—oldest consecutively run professional rodeo in Kansas

New Mexico State Championship Ranch Rodeo Invitational—near Red River, New Mexico

Prescott Frontier Days—Prescott, Arizona

Reno Rodeo—Reno, Nevada

Rocky Mountain Stampede—Greeley, Colorado

Rodeo de Santa Fe—Santa Fe, New Mexico

July

Calgary Stampede—Calgary, Alberta, Canada

Cheyenne Frontier Days—Cheyenne, Wyoming

Cody Nite Rodeo—Cody, Wyoming

Corn Palace Stampede Rodeo—Mitchell, South Dakota

Days of 47 Rodeo—Salt Lake City, Utah

Five Star Championship Rodeo—Davie, Florida

August

Cody Nite Rodeo—Cody, Wyoming

Dodge City Round-Up Rodeo—Dodge City, Kansas

Mesquite Championship Rodeo—Mesquite, Texas

September

Kingaroy—Queensland, Australia

Pendleton Round-Up—Pendleton, Oregon

Southern New Mexico State Fair Ranch Rodeo—Las Cruces, New Mexico

October

Professional Bull Riding Finals—Las Vegas, Nevada

Roswell Ranch Rodeo—Roswell, New Mexico

November

    Professional Bull Riding Championship—Las Vegas, Nevada

    Working Ranch Cowboys Rodeo Championship—Amarillo, Texas

December

    Wrangler National Finals Rodeo—Las Vegas, Nevada

Rodeo Associations

Listed below in alphabetical order are only a few of the myriad of worldwide rodeo associations. These are some of the well-known and not so well-known groups.

    Australian Bushmen's Campdraft and Rodeo Association

    Australian Professional Rodeo Association

    Canadian Professional Rodeo Association

    European Cowboy Rodeo Association

    International Professional Rodeo Association

    National Rodeo Association in Caboolture, Queensland, Australia

    Okinawa Bull Riding Association, Japan

    Professional Bull Riding Association

    Professional Rodeo Cowboys Association

    Southwest Indian Rodeo Association

    Working Ranch Cowboys Association

    Women's Professional Rodeo Association

Fig. 14.1.
Patriotism is an important part of rodeo. At this Silver City,
New Mexico, rodeo, contestants proudly display the American flag.
PHOTO BY HALEY CRAWFORD.

14

Did You Know? Bits of Trivia

- Texas officially designated rodeo the state sport in 1997.
- Bulls don't charge at the color red. They're color blind. They charge because they see something moving.
- The first indoor rodeo was held at the Fort Worth Cowtown Coliseum—in 1918. It was billed as "strictly a contest," and included ladies' bucking broncs, junior steer wrestling, men's steer wrestling, and bucking broncs.
- The first live radio broadcast of a rodeo was on the National Broadcasting Company network, from Texas—1932.
- The forerunner organization of the 4-H Club formed in 1913—the Baby Beef Club.
- The Cowboy Hall of Fame in Oklahoma City, Oklahoma, changed its name in 2000 to the National Cowboy and Western Heritage Museum.
- Eight seconds was selected for roughstock events because the first eight seconds are the animal's best efforts. After that time, he tends to tire. Since half the roughstock points are based on the animal, cowboys want that animal to buck his best.
- Bronc riding rules have changed since the days when they could do anything to hold on. In the 1800s, they often carried a quirt to urge the horse a

little, and they fanned the bronc with their hat. Now they hold on with one hand and leave the other free.

- The word *rodeo* was first used in 1924 in connection with the Prescott (Arizona) Frontier Days. Rodeos were billed as Cowboy Tournaments, Wild West Shows, Fiestas, Cowboy Carnivals, Rangeland Sports, Round-Ups, Shows, or Gatherings.
- The Humane Society banned the use of spurs in 1910. However, the Rodeo Committee disagreed and insisted that it would stand behind its members—even going to jail if their contestants were arrested.
- The Cowgirl Hall of Fame is located in Fort Worth, Texas.
- The average bucking horse or bull works less than five minutes per year in the arena.
- Human skin is 1–2mm thick, horsehide is 5mm, and bull hide is 7mm thick.
- In 1935, Earl and Weldon Bascom produced Columbia, Mississippi's first rodeo—now declared to be the first night rodeo held outdoors under electric lights.

Fig. 14.2.
Children as young as three start their rodeo careers on sheep, then graduate up to steers.
PHOTO BY HALEY CRAWFORD.

Fig. 14.3.
Bulls live a life of leisure in the rodeo world.
PHOTO BY HALEY CRAWFORD.

- Bulls will dig huge holes in the ground with their hooves and horns. Some holes are big enough for them to sit in and be level with the ground.
- Between 1930 and 1941, only fifty women competed in rodeos. When World War II started, the number of rodeos declined, and by 1942 only twenty-six women competed.
- Cheyenne Frontier Days usually brings in over eighteen hundred contestants. The trademark phrase for this rodeo, "Daddy of 'em All," was coined in 1919 when Cheyenne gained worldwide recognition for having the biggest rodeo in the West.

Fig. 15.1.
Nothing says "cowboy" more than chaps, boots, and stirrups.
Photo by Bert Entwistle.

15

Glossary—They Said What?

Barrier

The barrier is a rope or nylon strung across the front of the box where the roper or steer wrestler waits for his stock to be released. The barrier allows the cattle to have a calculated head start. Distance depends on the size of the arena. The barrier is connected to the stock with a breakaway rope and when the animal reaches the "advantage point," the rope releases and the barrier in front of the cowboy falls to the side. If the rider "breaks" the barrier, he is assessed a ten-second penalty, which usually eliminates his chance to win.

Brands

Branding dates back at least from 2700 B.C. Paintings in Egyptian tombs show oxen being branded. The ancient Greeks and Romans marked livestock and slaves alike with hot irons. Hernando Cortez introduced the practice and art of branding in the New World in 1541. His brand was three crosses.

Nothing has ever replaced the definitive   mark of ownership better than a brand. Brands nowadays are registered with state livestock boards. Most calves look alike, so an unbranded animal, a "slick," is almost impossible to legally identify except by a brand. The most popular locations for brands on animals are the right or left hip or shoulder.

Brands are much like hieroglyphics. They may contain letters, numbers, pictures, and/or characters. Any combination. They are read just like a book—left to right, top to bottom.

Want your own brand? Choose a brand as simple as possible. Most brands need to be three characters due to the number of already registered brands. Avoid closed characters such as a Q, B, or 8—they tend to blotch. The branding irons themselves are a work of art. Made out of iron, the face (characters) should be at least four inches high and three-eighths of an inch wide, which creates a good brand. When heated, they should not be red-hot, but the color of ashes. This makes a clean brand.

One consideration when branding. Don't brand a wet or damp animal. The brand will scald, leaving a block, a sore, or no brand at all. Good branding sears the

Fig. 15.2.
All rodeo livestock is branded. Note brands on rump and shoulder. This cowboy's free arm is not touching the horse. Note the flank strap under the horse's flank.
Photo by Myke Groves.

Fig. 15.3.
Putting on chaps
requires a bit of
twisting and turning,
not unlike riding
roughstock.
PHOTO BY
HALEY CRAWFORD.

hair and the outer layer of skin. When the branding iron is lifted, the brand should be the color of saddle leather.

Visit the Internet for more about branding.

Chaps

These protective leather or suede leg coverings have been in use as long as cowboys have been around. Bull riders wear slick chaps so that horns and hoofs will slide off more easily. They wear chaps with fringe as the flapping makes the ride look even more exciting than it already is. Bronc riders wear rough chaps, usually made of suede, which gives their legs a better grip.

Chinks are the short chaps, usually fringed, and hit just below the knee. Shotgun chaps are tight fitting, similar to jeans, and go to the ankle. In 1926, Earl Bascom (1906–1995) designed and made rodeo's first high-cut riding chaps, which are in standard use today.

Dally

A team roper or tie-down roper wraps his rope around the saddle horn two times, securing one end of his rope to the saddle. The saddle horn, which is usually three and a half inches high, is padded and wrapped with leather and then encased in rubber to keep the rope from rubbing the horn too much and damaging the leather. A long weekend of roping will cause the rope to cut through the rubber. A good garden hose provides a great wrap for the horn.

Flank Strap

This leather strap covered in sheepskin fleece is secured with a buckle and snugged up under the animal's belly as the bronc or bull leaves the chute. Horses and bulls are naturally sensitive in their flank area, therefore use of the strap encourages the animal to extend his back legs when trying to get his rider on the ground. It is never placed over the genitalia and does not cause pain. If pulled too tight, or left too loose, the strap loses its effectiveness. The "flankman" is responsible for knowing how tight to pull it so that the horse or bull bucks well.

Foul—Re-ride

In saddle bronc and bareback riding, the judges will allow a re-ride, if they believe that the horse interfered with the cowboy's attempt to position himself on that first important jump. A re-ride is also allowed if the horse smashes the rider against the chute when the gate opens, or if he bumps the chute corner on the way out. The "back" judge, the judge closest to the chutes, decides this call. A re-ride may be awarded if the bronc stalls when the gate is opened.

The re-ride option allows the cowboy a chance to gain points that he otherwise wouldn't obtain. However, if he's been awarded points and given a re-ride, those points are wiped off the scoreboard. If he doesn't make the eight seconds, he receives no score at all. His decision for a re-ride is complex.

Free Hand

All roughstock events (bull riding, saddle bronc, and bareback), require the use of only one hand. The other "free" hand is held out to one side and may not touch the animal, the cowboy, or his equipment. Disqualification results if it does.

Go Round

This is a cowboy's timed ride in a rodeo event. All contestants in a certain event are in the go round. The "short go" refers to the championship turn where only a few cowboys ride.

Fig. 15.4.
Rubbing a hand up and down the resin-coated bull rope
creates a sticky surface, which gives the cowboy a better grip.
PHOTO BY HALEY CRAWFORD.

Marking Out

In saddle bronc and bareback riding, both spurs have to be touching the bronc's shoulders until the horse's feet hit the ground after the initial move from the chute. A rider who fails to do this is disqualified. This is the first thing judges watch for.

Piggin' String

This six-inch rope is clenched in the tie-down roper's teeth as he waits in the box. Once the calf is released and he lassoes the animal, he wraps any three feet with the piggin' string. The spelling never has a "g" at the end. Believed originally to have been referred to as a "pegging string," this modern derivation is much more colorful.

Rank

Rank refers to stock that excels above and beyond the other roughstock. Rank bulls are usually reserved for the seasoned riders. Rank bulls are the toughest of the tough.

Resin

Resin is the sticky substance used by the roughstock rider (bull, saddle broncs, and bareback) to make his glove grip the rope more securely. Resin is rubbed on the glove and up and down the bull rope. Rubbing creates friction, which in turn makes the resin sticky. Too much resin may result in the cowboy's hand sticking in his rigging, possibly resulting in serious injury.

Spurs

More than a tool, more than a prized possession or even an heirloom, the spur is a symbol of the American West. A misunderstood implement, many people see spurs as ghastly torture instruments designed to inflict pain on helpless animals. Such treatment, however, would be the farthest thing from the mind of any skilled cowboy, whether in the West of today or a century ago.

A cowboy's horse is an indispensable partner and, in most cases, an important part of his life. Riders use spurs to cue the mounts while they themselves do complex tasks in the saddle such as roping.

The spur has been a part of the horseman's outfit dating back to 700 B.C., centuries before the invention of the stirrup.

Spurs have always identified their wearers as horsemen, a distinction that, in virtually all societies, sets them apart.

As the cattle industry in the West evolved, so did regional styles in cowboy equipment. The early cowboys wore spurs of Mexican design since very little

Fig. 15.5.
Spurs come in all shapes and sizes. These
blunt rowels are very popular. Note the fancy stirrup.
<small>PHOTO BY AUTHOR.</small>

else was available. These were heavy and soon gave way to lighter, almost military styles.

During the heyday of the Texas cattle drives, from the 1860s to 1880s, mass-produced spurs that sold for about two dollars a pair were the only spurs available on the plains.

Spurs are generally stamped with the maker's name on the heel band. Overlaid decorations of silver, brass, and copper are soldered in hundreds of designs. Steer heads, stars, snakes, hearts, dice, leaves, arrows, and birds are popular. Some cowboys have their brand, initials, or nickname added to the heel band.

The growing popularity of rodeo also has created a market for specialized riding spurs as well as larger fancier ones for parades and Wild West Shows. The demand for modern spurs is growing rapidly as the art form grows along with the interest in rodeo.

A Biographical Note By the Author

> There's absolutely nothing better than getting on top
> of that ol' bull, gripping the rope, and nodding your head.
> —Melody Groves

Few things happen that change your life forever. Sure, there's births, deaths, even natural disasters—but there's nothing quite like sitting on the back of a one-ton bull, that heat radiating into your body, that somehow makes you stare into your very soul. From there on, nothing is ever the same.

Growing up in southern New Mexico, I attended rodeos whenever possible and even headed toward a barrel-racing career. Plans got sidetracked when my family and I moved to the Philippines for three years. By the time I returned to the United States, the future took a different turn, but my love for anything rodeo and western still burned.

I didn't pursue rodeo as a sport, career, or hobby until a few years ago. But my rides on those bulls just fueled the fire for more. While further bull riding has been curtailed due to injuries, I still live rodeo through my novels and my participation in an Old West reenactors group, the New Mexico Gunfighters, in Albuquerque, New Mexico.

So, with deep respect and admiration for rodeo cowboys/cowgirls, I tip my hat to you.

—Melody Groves

For Melody Groves's books of historical fiction—*The Quest* and *Sonoran Rage*—visit http://www.melodygroves.com; books may be ordered there or on Xlibris.com. She writes fiction under the pen name Mesa Dean.

Index